Vertical Challenge

*F*irst prototype of the longest-produced piston helicopter series in history, the Hiller 360X takes to the air early in 1948. The bulbous cabin and underslung stabilizer were unique to this prototype.

Vertical Challenge

The Hiller Aircraft Story

Jay P. Spenser

University of Washington Press

Seattle & London

Copyright © 1992 by
the University of Washington Press
Printed in the United States of America
Designed by Audrey Meyer

Library of Congress Cataloging-in-Publication
Data
Spenser, Jay P.
    Vertical challenge : the Hiller Aircraft
story / Jay P. Spenser.
      p. cm.
    Includes bibliographical references and
index.
    ISBN 0-295-97203-3
    1. Hiller Aircraft Company—History.
2. Helicopter industry—United States—
History. I. Title.
HD9711.25.U64H557   1992
338.7′629133352′0973—dc20   92-7525
                          CIP

April 1949. The first civil helicopter to cross the United States lands at the foot of Wall Street in Manhattan. Flying the last leg of the tour himself, Stanley Hiller, Jr., is at the controls.

For Deborah *and* Brian

*T*he three Hiller HJ-1 Hornets
hover in echelon.

*T*he Navy's Hiller HOE-1s in formation
at Palo Alto (overleaf).

Contents

*F*our different Hiller helicopters hover over the ramp at Palo Alto in 1957. Seen from nearest to farthest are a YROE-1 Rotorcycle, a YH-32A ULV Sally Rand, an Army YH-23C, and a 12-C.

***S**tanley Hiller, Jr., at an idyllic moment, demonstrating a potential use of personal helicopters on his float-equipped XH-44.*

Illustrations

Acknowledgments

I extend my most heartfelt appreciation to Stanley Hiller, Jr., who made available primary source material, consented to be interviewed, and helped locate others who might shed light on a company that ceased to exist a quarter of a century ago. The archives of the Hiller Aircraft Museum yielded reports, company newspapers, promotional literature, photographic negatives, and many other materials invaluable to the completion of this book.

Special thanks also go to former Hiller Aircraft Company officers, engineers, pilots, and employees, notably Everett ("Curly") Barrick, the late Robert Boughton, Chuck Carel, Richard Cutter, Warren Galliano, Bruce Jones, Harvey Holm, Al Hutain, Phil Johnston, Harold Lemont, Rose Lesslie, Dick Peck, Warren Rockwell, Elbert Sargent, A. W. B. Vincent, Langhorne Washburn, and—for countless hours of singularly valuable help—Wayne Wiesner. In addition to information and materials, they provided insight into what was a unique and exciting corporate environment. For the lion's share of photographs illustrating this volume, belated thanks go to company photographer H. W. ("Wick") Wichers.

Materials, expertise, and invaluable assistance were also rendered by Leo Bellieu, Linda Bennett, Regina Burns at the Army Aviation Museum, John Greenwood, Bill Hartford, Joe Mashman, senior rotary-wing engineer/historian John Schneider of Boeing Helicopters, Delford Smith of Evergreen International Airlines, Joe Soloy, Dick Tipton and Bell Helicopter Textron, John Williams of San Mateo College, Bell Model 47 inventor Arthur Young, and John Zugschwert and the American Helicopter Society. Tudor Huddleston, Elizabeth Otis, and others provided information, for which I am grateful.

At the National Air and Space Museum, Smithsonian Institution, I am indebted to Mark Avino, Trish Graboske, Dr. Von Hardesty, Dale Hrabak, Russell Lee, Donald Lopez, Dr. Robert van der Linden, and Larry Wilson. At the Museum of Flight in Seattle, I thank Mark Smith. I also thank former executive director Howard Lovering and former staff member Virginia Wagner.

Finally, gratitude is extended to the University of Washington Press—and in particular to acquisitions editor Don Cioeta, manuscript editor Gretchen Van Meter, and art director Audrey Meyer for the physical realization of this book. I feel fortunate indeed for this pleasurable and productive association.

*A*head of its time, the innovative Hiller J-10 was developed but not completed in 1946 for a personal-helicopter market that never materialized. The above craft is actually a 1991 replica built for display at the Hiller Museum. The original two-seat J-10 counteracted rotor torque with compressed air.

Vertical Challenge

Introduction

It was like Wilbur and Orville all over again," Frank Coffyn often said of the early Hiller Aircraft Company.[1] He would know; thirty-six years before joining Hiller in 1946, Coffyn learned to fly under the Wright brothers and went on to demonstrate their flying machines to an amazed public.

In the Hiller Aircraft Company, Frank Coffyn witnessed a similar development process. Stanley Hiller, Jr.—who built and flew his own helicopter by 1944—and his small team set their sights on the commercial helicopter business with scarcely more real support than the Wrights had enjoyed in their quest. Woefully little information on helicopters existed in print, particularly "hard" engineering data. Worse still, Sikorsky and the few other centers of helicopter development were all back East, too far from the California-based company to be of much help. Finally, the two camps one might have expected to champion this new form of flight—autogyro manufacturers like Pitcairn and Kellett, and major fixed-wing aircraft companies like Douglas or Lockheed—provided minimal leadership; the helicopter, it appeared at the close of World War II, was still the largely unwanted stepchild of aviation.

Not so to Stanley Hiller. Hoping to exploit a widely heralded postwar market for personal helicopters—a market that never materialized—he began work in 1942 against seemingly overwhelming odds and attained volume production of a successful commercial helicopter before the decade was out. The Hiller 360—history's first stable production helicopter—differs from those of other successful manufacturers in that it arose entirely as a private venture, belying the oft-repeated view that all development in this field was the result of military spending.

The Bell Model 47—the industry's first production civil helicopter—enjoyed government support, albeit indirectly. Developed by mathematician Arthur Young and his small team in the early and mid-1940s, this excellent helicopter was financed with profits from World War II sales of P-39s and other Bell military aircraft. The company's postwar contracts in support of U.S. Air Force/National Advisory Committee for Aeronautics (NACA) high-speed flight research added a boost of a promotional nature: when Captain Charles E. Yeager shattered the sound barrier in his Bell X-1 rocket plane on 14 October 1947, the Bell 47 inevitably rode the X-1's coattails.

Despite an estimated 300 helicopter projects in the United States during and just after World War II (the vast majority never giving rise to flying prototypes), only four companies—Sikorsky, Bell, Piasecki, and Hiller—actually achieved volume production before the end of the 1940s. Hiller Aircraft, which built the first successful helicopter west of the Mississippi River, was the third company to receive an approved type certificate for helicopter production in the United States.

But manufacturing helicopters is only one part of Hiller Aircraft's astonishing twenty-five-year history of creativity. Flying platforms, flying jeeps, and flying submarines; ramjet helicopters and mammoth aerial cranes with jet engines at their rotor tips; tilt-wing transport planes capable of taking off and landing vertically; wingless battlefield-resupply aircraft designed to hug the ground at Mach 1 and land in their own length—the list of flying machines proposed or actually built by Hiller Aircraft often reads more like science fiction than fact.

Amazingly, the craft mentioned above could all have flown, and many did, with technology available in the 1950s and early 1960s. First in the vertical flight industry with a separate engineering think tank akin to Lockheed's famous Skunk Works, Hiller Aircraft made research and development, along with helicopter production, its life's blood to compensate for its newness, small size, and lack of war-won capital.

Of the military services, the U.S. Army was the logical customer for Hiller Aircraft. Hiller's creativity found little support within that service, however, because those with an understanding of aviation and aerial requirements had left when the Army Air Forces became the separate U.S. Air Force in 1947. Much of what might have been, therefore, never progressed beyond the proposal or prototype stage.

Hiller produced military and commercial helicopters for fifteen years in healthy competition with Bell Helicopters. Then in the mid-1960s, a new competitor disrupted the light helicopter industry by subverting the legitimate procurement process and thereby stealing, in effect, the contract for the Army's milestone light observation helicopter (LOH). With this theft, Hughes Tool Company's Aircraft Division drove Hiller's Palo Alto company out of business. In an ironic twist of fate, Stanley Hiller would himself in later years engineer a successful takeover to save a then-ailing Hughes Tool Company.

Hiller Aircraft has left a legacy disproportionate to its small size. In addition to a line of excellent production helicopters, its talented team of engineers generated imaginative flight concepts. Huge flying cranes with jet engines at the tips of their rotor blades, ducted-fan flying machines, vertical-takeoff-and-landing (VTOL) intercity airliners, and other as-yet-unrealized aviation possibilities bear this company's distinctive stamp to varying degrees. These efforts to change the face of aviation across a quarter-century make Hiller Aircraft a fascinating case study within the vertical flight industry.

Adventurous Beginnings

Stanley Hiller, Jr., became intrigued by helicopters early in 1940 while he was still in high school. Researching this new form of flight in his free time over the next year, he gathered what sparse information San Francisco's public libraries, its technical bookstores, and the region's universities could provide. Like the articles in the mechanics and aviation magazines he had grown up reading—most of which predicted that Americans would soon fly their own personal helicopters—what he found ranged from the historical to the fanciful; little was to be had of a technical nature.

Everywhere he looked, Hiller found clippings on Igor I. Sikorsky and the experimental VS-300 helicopter he first flew late in 1939. Photographs showed the fifty-year-old inventor, attired in overcoat and homburg, hovering his much-modified testbed at his Vought-Sikorsky plant in Stratford, Connecticut. Although of minimal technical help, these clippings firmed the resolve of the young Californian to develop and market small helicopters of his own.

If the odds against success were long, Stanley Hiller was nevertheless uniquely qualified. His great-grandfather had settled in California in 1849, establishing a tradition of hardy self-reliance that Hiller's father, Stanley Hiller, Sr., brought to another frontier as a noted inventor and one of northern California's pioneer aviators.

Born on 15 November 1924, Stanley Hiller, Jr., learned to use tools at an early age in his father's well-equipped workshop. Although he displayed a decided mechanical aptitude, the younger Hiller decided early in life that business would be his calling. This decision stemmed in large measure from observing his father working with his business partner. Although the former had the ideas, it was the latter who devised ways to apply and exploit them. Business intrigued the inventor's son, who perceived a valuable instrument for change.

In 1937, having lost a balsa-wood-and-tissue model airplane to a crash, he salvaged its little gasoline engine and put it in a model race car of his own design. Demand quickly outstripped his ability to build others for his friends, and then for their friends, so in 1940 he founded Hiller Industries to undertake large-scale assembly-line manufacture of the "Hiller Comet" for national distribution.

To form sleek metal bodies for his racers, Hiller helped perfect a method of die-casting nonferrous metals like aluminum. With the coming of World War II, Hiller Industries used this new process to make airframe parts—the first aircraft components so manufactured—for military aircraft rolling off West Coast assembly lines. Hiller's C-47 window frames and A-26 control pedestals, for example, were stronger and lighter than the steel units they replaced.

America's entry into the war was still some months away, however, when Hiller began devoting his time to preliminary design of a helicopter. To refine his ideas, he built models and dropped them off tall buildings after stationing friends with cameras at windows on different floors to photograph them on the way down. Another substitute for a wind tunnel was Hiller's Buick convertible, which, modified with a teststand for models, simulated low-speed flight with some degree of success.

When after six months the preliminary design was finished, Hiller left the University of California and sold Hiller Industries in order to form Hiller Aircraft. His first employee was Harold Sigler, a naval architect who had worked for Hiller Industries. Fortyish, wiry, a fine draftsman and self-taught maritime engineer who worked quickly and often intuitively, Sigler set about producing a detailed design for the as-yet-unnamed helicopter. "He was an extraordinary talent," Stanley Hiller recalled of him, "a brilliant man in his field."[1]

Two other remarkable individuals filled out the ranks of Hiller Aircraft in 1942. The first was Jack Galliano, sixtyish, a true craftsman in the Old-World tradition who could form perfect compound curves in metal with nothing more than a ham-

mer and a bag of sand. The second was Bert Cann, a burly welder in his midthirties who had honed his skills in the Kaiser Shipyards of Richmond, California. Both men were jacks-of-all-trades who could build almost anything. Galliano in particular had a genius for machining parts from scratch.

If lack of aviation expertise hindered the small company, it also had a positive effect. Having no contact with the East Coast rotary-wing community, autogyro or helicopter, and without even an aeronautical engineer participating in the design, Hiller Aircraft was uniquely free to pursue fresh and unconventional approaches to the problems of helicopter flight.

In a rare instance of the right people coming together at the right time in history, the four men set to work in Galliano's automobile repair garage in Oakland, California. The small facility was already overcrowded—Galliano subsidized his income by building midget race cars on the premises. Luckily, the garage also had a machine shop with an antiquated lathe, drill press, milling machine, and other equipment of post–industrial revolution vintage driven by belts from shafts spinning overhead. In this tinkerer's paradise, work began in December 1942 on a machine very different from other successful helicopters developed in the United States.

Called the XH-44 Hiller-copter (the designation denoted "experimental Hiller" and the year it would fly), the unusual craft taking shape featured two opposite-turning rotors on the same central shaft. It would in fact be the first successful helicopter with "rigid" rotors

A *helicopter unlike any other nears*
completion early in 1943. Engineer
Harold Sigler (left) and Stanley Hiller,
Jr., stand on the XH-44's steel tube
frame.

(meaning that the blades were not hinged at the hub as was universally the case with rotary wing craft of that era) and the first successful helicopter to employ rotor blades of all-metal construction.

The idea of hinged, limp, overly flexible rotors such as were used on autogyros and other helicopters had not appealed to Hiller, who from the outset considered them a potential source of trouble. In a departure from accepted standards, he and Harold Sigler instead settled upon totally rigid all-metal rotors because they promised higher speeds and permitted closer spacing between the rotor heads. As these new rotors were subject to higher flight loads than were conventional rotors, Sigler performed stress calculations, which, in retrospect, were extremely rudimentary and failed to take into account vibratory loads. The resulting helicopter nevertheless emerged hell-for-stout, its rotors clearly up to the job.

A twin-rotor coaxial machine then appeared to be more efficient than single-rotor designs, which require tail rotors to offset torque, the force trying to spin them in the direction opposite to the rotation of their own rotors. Tail rotors, Hiller knew, consumed 10 percent or more of the power generated by a helicopter's engine, power that might otherwise help lift and propel the helicopter. Coaxial helicopters, in contrast, need no tail rotor because each main rotor cancels out the torque of the other.

A coaxial configuration permitted a more compact design; with no tail rotor there was no need for a long tail boom, thereby offsetting to a degree the extra weight of two rotors. Control was also simplified because all linkages and lines were clustered in the center.

A coaxial configuration also avoided the tendency of single-rotor helicopters to roll during high-speed flight. A rotor's advancing blades combine their own rotational speed with the helicopter's forward airspeed to produce increased lift on one side of the rotor; the retreating blades, in contrast, subtract their rotational speed from the helicopter's forward airspeed and produce less lift. The resulting asymmetrical lift at high speed produces an uncontrollable roll, which lasts until forward airspeed is reduced. Coaxial helicopters avoid this problem because their rotors turn simultaneously in opposite directions, presenting an equal number of advancing and retreating blades on each side.

Fourth and most important, the Hiller team settled on the coaxial configuration simply because it was different. Hiller's business instincts told him that, without something the public could readily discern as being innovative, his little company would fail to emerge from Igor Sikorsky's shadow. And a giant shadow it was.

Public fascination with Igor Sikorsky's activities on the banks of Connecticut's Housatonic River had given rise to the widespread misconception that he had actually invented the helicopter. In truth, as Hiller knew from his research, the Russian expatriate deserved credit not for its invention but for realizing its first practical application in the Army's R-4 as the first helicopter ever produced in number. Even its configuration as finally worked out in the VS-300—a single main

A proud team poses with the completed Hiller XH-44. Left to right: Jack Galliano and son Jack Jr., Harold Sigler, Stan Hiller, Bert Cann, and a painter hired to apply finishing touches.

rotor with a small vertical tail rotor to offset torque—was not Sikorsky's invention. Russian experimenter Boris N. Yuriev employed this on his unsuccessful helicopter of 1912; so did Dutchman A. G. von Baumhauer in his marginally flyable helicopter of the latter 1920s.

Gentle and deferential, Igor Sikorsky himself frequently sought to set the record straight, but two factors beyond his control defeated him. The first was a skillful media promotion of his work orchestrated by the United Aircraft Corporation (today United Technologies), the powerful consortium of which Sikorsky Aircraft remains a member to this day. The second factor, ironically, was Igor Sikorsky's own fame. The first person in history to build and fly a multiengine airplane, the aviation pioneer constructed giant biplanes for Imperial Russia during World War I and—having immigrated to the United States after the revolution—further enhanced his reputation by building Pan American Airways' first four-engine flying boats in the early 1930s.

Despite his success in the fixed-wing field, helicopters remained Igor Sikorsky's abiding love. His steadfast interest (dating back to two unsuccessful attempts to build one in 1909 and 1910) evoked the cherished American archetype of success by dint of persistent effort. The citizens of Sikorsky's adopted country, in short, were predisposed to mythify him as sole inventor of the helicopter, whatever the truth of the matter.

Stanley Hiller's determination not to follow in Igor Sikorsky's footsteps was vindicated by the low-slung craft with a light tubular framework expertly welded by Bert Cann. Countering general ideas of how a helicopter should look, it was a blunt-nosed teardrop ending rakishly with a spike instead of an extended tail boom.

Because of the war, Hiller's group was forced to make items like fairleads and turnbuckles that would otherwise have been available off the shelf at the local airport. A more crippling shortage by far was the lack of a power plant, wartime priorities having reserved light plane engines for other uses. No engine meant no helicopter, and no helicopter would soon spell the end of the young company whose means were already stretched to the limit.

In an effort to resolve this problem, Stanley Hiller made several trips to Wright Field in Dayton, Ohio, in the spring of 1943 to meet with Colonel Frank Gregory, head of the U.S. Army Air Forces' fledgling helicopter program. With monies appropriated under the landmark Dorsey Bill of 1938, Gregory (a former autogyro pilot) had fostered development of both the unsuccessful Platt-LePage XR-1 and the eminently successful Sikorsky VS-316.

Although he was impressed with the young man who knew so much about helicopters, Gregory was steadfast in his refusal to help Hiller obtain an engine. Still, these trips were not wasted—the Californian saw at close range the Army's YR-4s, as the Sikorsky VS-316 was designated in military service. The world's first production helicopter, the R-4 was the first helicopter Stan Hiller had ever seen.

Hiller also traveled to Washington, D.C. Wartime priorities being in effect, he spent the three-day train trip standing

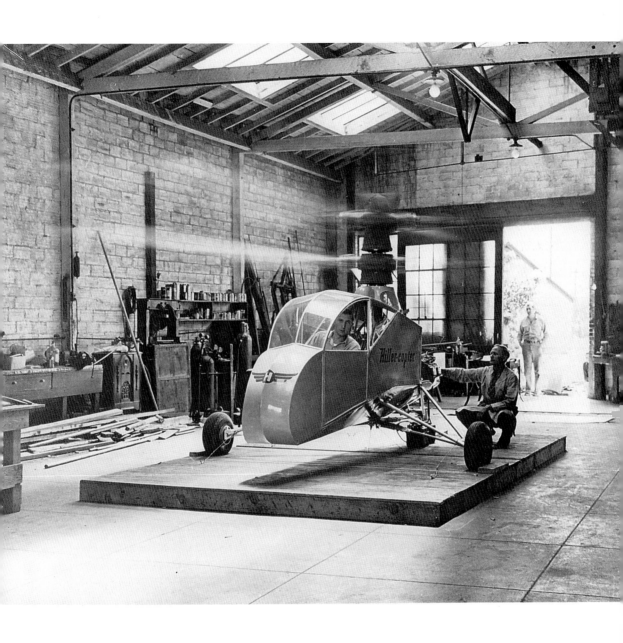

*H*iller runs up the finished XH-44 late in 1943. A moment later, when he applied pitch to the restrained craft's rotors, all the skylights were sucked from the ceiling of Jack Galliano's automobile repair garage.

or sitting on his suitcase, carefully guarding his quarter-scale one-hundred-pound model of the XH-44's coaxial rotor system. Wind, rain, a wartime lack of public transportation, and startled looks greeted him as he made the rounds of indifferent and unresponsive agencies in the nation's capital.

In fact, it took several trips and months of rejection before Hiller finally found an office of the War Production Board interested in his efforts. A. W. Lewis, head of the Aircraft Priorities Division, thought enough of the XH-44 to arrange a meeting for Hiller with rotary-wing experts of the National Advisory Committee for Aeronautics (NACA). With Lewis's help, the necessary priorities were eventually granted, and Hiller Aircraft was free to purchase a 90-hp Franklin air-cooled engine.

The XH-44 was finished late in 1943. It was fastened firmly to the floor of Jack Galliano's shop in Oakland, which Hiller Aircraft had rented. Stan Hiller climbed aboard for a first static run. After the rotors had come up to speed, he pulled the collective lever to apply pitch to the blades. The XH-44 sucked in all the building's skylights in an explosion of glass—proof indeed that the Hiller-copter was ready and eager to fly.

At that time Hiller Aircraft was very close to going completely broke, so hiring a professional test pilot was out of the question, even if one with rotary-wing experience could have been found. Hiller was the only member of the company with any training—he had learned to fly fixed-wing aircraft in the mid-1930s—but this scarcely prepared him to fly the XH-44, particularly as his father's

1929 Stinson bore no similarity to his team's untried one-of-a-kind contraption. But the pragmatic company president rose to this challenge as he had to all the others. "It seemed to all of us," Hiller later observed, "that if we could build it, we could fly it."[2]

Cooling problems, trouble aligning the reduction gears, and other difficulties delayed the first attempt at tethered flight until early 1944. On this less-than-auspicious occasion, the yellow machine lifted off the ground, settled laterally, and rolled over with a loud bang as the blade tips struck the ground. A single restraining cable attached to the underside of the machine precipitated the accident, but its underlying cause was the fact that the pilot had to teach himself to fly a helicopter during the course of testing.

Ironically, had the Hiller team used rotors of conventional construction (hinged blades made of wooden ribs over steel tubing, all covered with doped fabric), the crash would have deformed the hinges and shattered the blades. Lacking money for all-new rotors, Hiller Aircraft would have been out of business. As it was, though, the XH-44's ambitious rigid rotor with all-metal blades saved the day; however badly twisted they looked, damage to these blades was confined to the tips. Just enough money remained from the sale of Hiller's model race car business to effect repairs and try again.

With a better restraint system consisting of three long cables attached to the XH-44's landing-gear struts, tethered tests resumed in Memorial Stadium at the University of California's Berkeley campus. The stadium provided shelter from the wind and, with its gates locked, relief

A *first attempt at tethered flight at Hiller's family home in Berkeley ends abruptly early in 1944. Pilot inexperience and improper restraining cables caused the accident. Fortunately, the XH-44's robust metal blades were repairable.*

from the huge crowds invariably attracted by the then-novel helicopter. After much tinkering—and after having learned to control his machine—Stanley Hiller performed its first free flight on 4 July 1944.

No surging crowd, no throng of reporters, and no contingent of emergency vehicles were on hand to mark the moment when Hiller, casually attired in a T-shirt, lifted the XH-44 into a hover, flew slowly forward, and then brought his yellow teardrop around in a wide circle to land where he had started. History had been made: the XH-44 was at once the first helicopter ever built and flown in the western United States and the first successful coaxial helicopter outside Europe.

Upon landing, Hiller looked up to the bleachers only to see one seat perplexingly empty. But just then Carolyn Balsdon's head popped up; the lovely young woman whom Hiller would marry in 1946 had not wanted to watch what promised to be an accident. Without brakes and with no directional control over his helicopter when not in the air, Hiller had rolled to a stop dangerously close to the stadium's goalposts. From the bleachers, it had looked as if the whirling rotors would surely strike them.

In its second free flight, the XH-44 stayed in the air for five minutes. Hiller's own perception of this flight was that it was almost as if a switch had been thrown, transforming the helicopter from a monster to an aircraft in which he could do no wrong. Thus encouraged, he decided to climb out of ground effect and treat the stadium like a racetrack. The successful new helicopter was now off and flying.

Hiller traveled East again armed with films of the Hiller-copter in flight to show to Lewis and the NACA's helicopter board. They arranged for him to see the Sikorsky HNS (the Navy designation of the R-4) then under development as the guest of Coast Guard Commander Frank A. Erickson at New York's Floyd Bennett Field. The experience convinced Hiller of the merits of his team's machine. Returning home, he resumed flight tests in Memorial Stadium and in rural areas of nearby Contra Costa County. Lewis and a prestigious entourage later made a pilgrimage to the San Francisco area specifically to observe these tests firsthand.

The Hiller-copter was demonstrated in public on 30 August 1944, at Beach Street and Marina Boulevard in San Francisco. Several hundred spectators, including government and military observers, watched as the pilot rose vertically in a stiff breeze to put the yellow craft through its paces. Adept by now in the intricate art of flying a helicopter, Hiller demonstrated circles, spun about the XH-44's vertical axis, moved forward and back, side to side, and otherwise thrilled the crowd before descending to settle gently on Marina Green. Cameras clicked and people cheered as he climbed out, but the international publicity and acclaim that followed did nothing to improve Hiller Aircraft's financial footing.

In a precision-landing demonstration at the Claremont Country Club the next day, Hiller placed one tire squarely on a handkerchief spiked to the grass. He then flew at Richmond Shipyard No. 3 to show the craft to wealthy shipbuilder and aviation enthusiast Henry J. Kaiser. Following a further demonstration in October 1944, during which the industrialist himself hovered the XH-44, Kaiser reportedly climbed out of the machine and exclaimed, "This is marvelous! We want to close the deal."[3]

Kaiser had earlier obtained support from the War Production Board for an unsuccessful helicopter-development program pursued at Fleetwings, an aircraft company he owned in Bristol, Pennsylvania. Acquiring rights to Hiller's remarkable helicopter presented Kaiser with an opportunity to save face, as well as a chance to pursue again his dream of an aircraft for every American household, then a popular vision of what the near future would hold.

Kaiser insisted that Hiller move to the Fleetwings factory in Pennsylvania—formerly the site of manufacture of lumbering Keystone bombers—but Hiller and company steadfastly refused to leave the San Francisco Bay area. In the end, Kaiser relented and an agreement was reached whereby Hiller Aircraft became the Hiller-copter Division of Kaiser Cargo.

Tests of the XH-44, meanwhile, revealed that the Hiller team's original control input estimates were low. Travel of the swashplate—the collar controlling the rotor heads—was consequently opened up to improve the prototype's handling. And controllable the Hiller-copter was, the minimal flex in its robust rotors giving maneuvers a uniquely crisp feel akin to wires under tension or a spring tightly wound. Instantly responsive and therefore demanding, the machine's flying characteristics neverthe-less proved straightforward—until, that is, the time came to perform tests of autorotation.

Autorotation to the ground is the maneuver that allows a helicopter to land safely in the event of an engine failure. Practiced by all helicopter pilots, it consists of placing the rotors (which automatically disengage from the drive shaft by means of a freewheeling clutch) in low pitch so that they windmill rapidly as the powerless craft descends. Near the ground, the pilot pulls up on the collective pitch lever to trade the rotor's stored inertia for momentary lift. This maneuver must be performed at the right height if the helicopter is to land gently; pull up either too soon or too late and the result is a crash.

For his autorotation test, Stanley Hiller selected a small private airstrip in the Sacramento Valley. The plan called for him to climb several hundred feet and, from a semihover, reduce power and rotor pitch while initiating a fairly steep dive. This test approached autorotation in the most dangerous way possible, with a realistic simulation to the ground instead of at high altitude with a descent to a predetermined level. By simulating an engine failure beginning with both minimum altitude and airspeed, Hiller unknowingly placed himself squarely in the middle of what aerodynamicists call the "dead man's curve," that infamous corner of the flight envelope where luck quickly runs out.

Halfway into the maneuver the aircraft began to twist wildly. Hiller corrected with opposite rudder—and the rotation suddenly increased. With options rapidly running out and nothing left to lose,

A revised tether keeps Hiller from
nosing over as he teaches himself to
fly helicopters in the University of
California's Memorial Stadium at
Berkeley.

Hiller tried reverse rudder—a control input that ordinarily would have accelerated the spin—and to his disbelief the XH-44 instantly stopped turning. Bringing in collective pitch and full power just before hitting the ground suddenly reversed the controls again, but Hiller stabilized just in time to make a passable landing.

Hiller later learned that this unsuspected characteristic of coaxial helicopters, a lurking danger waiting to strike, was rumored to have caused French pioneer Louis Breguet's coaxial helicopter to crash during an autorotation test in France in 1939. The pilot, who was not hurt, had reportedly failed to recognize that control reversal was to blame, and thus the cause was never published to warn later experimenters.

There would be other close calls for the XH-44. The dream of rooftop landings made the company's temporary quarters in Berkeley a tempting target. Late one afternoon after the day's regular flying was finished, a roof landing was staged for photographers to publicize this dramatic use of helicopters. The roof itself was less than ideal because it presented a slight incline at the touchdown point, so two Hiller engineers were stationed at either side of the landing zone to secure the machine as it came to rest.

Hiller touched down between two skylights and, leaving the rotors turning, stepped away from the machine as planned. Suddenly he realized the employees could not hold the XH-44, which began rolling inexorably toward the edge of the roof. He scrambled aboard and threw on full power just as the machine slid off the edge three stories

above ground. His rotors approaching the vertical, Hiller shot across a parking lot, barely cleared a fence, and sailed over a row of houses before bringing the helicopter safely to a hover a full block away. Less than two minutes later, a somewhat shaken but unhurt founder-cum-president-cum-test-pilot landed the craft on his helipad in the company lot and strolled away.

On another occasion, failure of the main gearbox instantly stopped the spinning rotors, but as luck would have it, the XH-44 was just moments away from what turned out to be a very jarring landing. Had the gearbox failed at altitude, the outcome would certainly have been fatal.

Having invested so much work in the bright yellow Hiller-copter and having survived so many memorable adventures with it, Hiller and his team looked on the sturdy single-seater with special affection: the helicopter seemed to forgive its builders their inexperience and to repay their enthusiasm with loyalty, combining the mettle of a thoroughbred horse with the faithfulness of a family dog. This experimental prototype had long since become more than just a machine to those who built it.

The versatile XH-44 was also an ideal testbed because it was designed to be easily modified. An accessible steel tube structure facilitated refinements and experimentation. The rotor assembly could be tilted forward and aft, the gap between the blades adjusted, and the swashplate changed to permit a full regimen of configurational studies. After flying for almost a year with completely rigid rotors, the XH-44 was modified in the spring of 1945 to incorporate teetering rigid rotors. The machine's 90-hp Franklin was also exchanged for a 125-hp four-cylinder Lycoming for improved performance, a change marked by the amended designation XH-44A.

The historic Hiller-copter flew until the end of 1945. Seven years later, its builder donated this historic prototype to the Smithsonian Institution in Washington, D.C., where it has been on display since the National Air and Space Museum opened in 1976.

Before the XH-44 quit flying, a dozen more employees arrived including draftsmen and engineers, many coming directly from the Kaiser Shipyards in Richmond, California. One key non-engineer from Kaiser was Bob Chambers, who became Hiller's chief financial officer. Chambers would later leave to help form Magna Engineering, the successful maker of an ingenious all-in-one home power-tool workshop called the Shopsmith.

A new arrival not from Kaiser was Edward Bennett, a civilian flight instructor who had spent much of the war training Army pilots. Because Bennett lacked rotary-wing experience and because Hiller was testing the company's one flyable machine, Bennett moved from flight-test duties—the basis on which he was hired—to a singularly valuable role as head of the experimental shop. Ed Bennett possessed mechanical skills bordering on genius; give him a crude sketch and in short order he would construct whatever was needed.

Work had begun in October 1944 on three Hiller X-2-235s, two-place metal-clad successors to the XH-44, each powered by a six-cylinder Lycoming engine rated at 235-hp. Where the XH-44 was the world's first successful rigid-rotor helicopter, the X-2-235s were super-rigid-rotor aircraft. Each of their blades could support a person standing at the tip without noticeable deflection. Ground tests of the first example began in the summer of 1945 at the old Berkeley Armory.

Although no specific military requirement yet existed for such a machine, the X-2-235 was intended primarily for U.S. Navy use in light utility, observation, and training roles. The Navy did not actually order the type, but it did procure the third uncompleted X-2-235 under the designation UH-1X for evaluation in NACA wind tunnels at Langley Field, Virginia. Vibration problems curtailed these tests for fear of damaging the wind tunnel, but not before results vindicated the Hiller group's belief in superrigid coaxial rotors as a valid approach to very high-speed helicopter flight.

The UH-1X (X-2-235) was Hiller's first military contract. It clearly ran counter to normal aircraft engineering, but then the team building it had experience only in designing ships, bridges, and similar beefy structures; the lack of even a single aeronautical engineer on Hiller's payroll to introduce that field's antipathy to heavy structures was, paradoxically, an advantage in the uncharted terrain being explored.

As a result of the NACA tests, Hiller initiated redesign of the X-2-235 to incorporate three-bladed coaxial rotors augmented by an aft-thrusting rear propeller. The reworked craft was obviously geared to flight at speeds substantially higher than those attained by existing helicopters. Main wheels retracting into

Hiller leaves his duties as company president to test another untried rotor system in spring 1945. Increased spacing between the much-modified prototype's rotors allowed installation of teetering blades to reduce loads and vibration.

*W*here the XH-44 had rigid rotors, the three X-2-235s had super-rigid rotors designed expressly for high-speed flight. The weight of a man at each tip scarcely deflects these blades. A proposed development of the X-2-235 was to have featured stub wings, retractable wheels, and a pusher propeller.

sleek wing stubs further confirmed this supposition. Meanwhile, the X-2-235s themselves had now progressed to tethered flight.

Late in 1944, meantime, the Office of Naval Research (ONR) had awarded Hiller a contract calling for development of a small, tethered helicopter platform. The company's second military contract specified a compact machine that would raise an emergency transmitter antenna some 300 feet into the air, that being the length of the tether.

In response, Hiller developed a tiny single-rotor machine called the Sky Hook. Disassembled, it fit into a tube just three feet long and six inches thick for easy stowage in life rafts. Power was supplied by a 1.1-hp gasoline engine. Torque compensation was ignored for the sake of simplicity; in flight, the Sky Hook's body rotated freely under its single rotor, its spin retarded somewhat by aerodynamic vanes.

The Navy evaluated Sky Hook in the fall of 1945. World War II having ended, however, there was little need for it, so the project was terminated. Hiller's Sky Hook was America's first gasoline-powered model helicopter ever to fly successfully.

A parting of the ways between Hiller and Kaiser some months later interrupted these projects. Precipitating the split was a carefully prepared Hiller-copter Division proposal calling for the expenditure of a million dollars, this being the amount Hiller calculated was needed to achieve helicopter production. Refusing to commit to so large an expenditure, Kaiser instead offered only to continue funding the Division at current levels.

It was clear to Hiller that helicopter manufacture would not be achieved anytime soon if his company remained within the Kaiser sphere. Accordingly, he declined the offer, and the association of these two men came to an amicable end. Of course, leaving the comfort of the vast Kaiser organization halted the regular influx of money to which Hiller and company had been accustomed for a year.

New financing was the first concern. It took two forms, immediate interim ("bridge") financing and, beyond that, a great deal more to cover design, development, and certification of a new helicopter, plus tooling for its production.

Money was only part of the challenge, however. Hiller had also to transform his organization from a division into a stand-alone company. The busy president found he must wear still more hats in an ever-expanding spectrum of duties. He had to talk to colleges, employment bureaus, and other institutions to get the personnel he needed. Just joining the corporate world entailed community activities and a host of other involvements. The cumulative demands were so great that Hiller soon understood why good division chiefs and general managers do not always make good chief executive officers.

Earlier experience running Hiller Industries and Hiller Aircraft now stood him in good stead, as did his observations from within the Kaiser organization. A greater asset still was Hiller's implicit faith in his own ability to create a successful company. He sensed strongly, moreover, that the time was right to pursue his dream of helicopter manufacture. At this juncture, his

A growing staff poses with the Hiller-copter in late 1945. Stanley Hiller's decision to forgo Kaiser financial support at year's end would reduce the number of employees by half.

capacity for bold yet realistic planning was critical to survival.

Meanwhile, Kaiser's love of aviation appeared to be waning. If so, he could be forgiven: the commendable Stearman-Hammond Y safety plane of the 1930s (a revised version of which he would briefly champion after World War II) never caught on. Having sold the government on huge wartime flying boats made of nonstrategic materials, moreover, Kaiser saw this cherished program's single development—Howard Hughes's mammoth HK-1 *Spruce Goose*—languish unfinished at war's end in a world now intent upon land-plane transportation. In addition, Kaiser had tried unsuccessfully to enlist military support for the wartime long-range flying-wing bomber proposed by Professor Otto Koppen of the Massachusetts Institute of Technology. And there was Kaiser's year-long stint as president of the troubled Brewster Aircraft Company; unable to resolve its labor difficulties, a frustrated Kaiser recommended instead that this manufacturer of Navy planes be shut down. Finally, as already stated, Henry Kaiser's helicopter project at Fleetwings in Pennsylvania had been a failure.

Perhaps for these reasons, an opportunity to acquire the Ford Motor Company's Willow Run factory—a huge Michigan facility built for license production of B-24 bombers during the war—gave Kaiser an alternate outlet for his considerable energies. The availability of this empty facility (America's most pro-ductive aircraft factory during the war) rekindled in the industrialist a long-standing desire to follow in the footsteps of Henry Ford. At that juncture, moreover, cars looked to be a safer investment than helicopters.

Accordingly, Henry Kaiser instead embarked on automobile production in collaboration with industry expert Joseph W. Frazer. Kaiser and Frazer automobiles (the latter a more luxurious, if equally bulbous, version of the former) began rolling off the assembly lines at Willow Run in 1946. This ill-conceived assault upon the giant auto makers lasted until 1953, when the struggling Kaiser-Frazer Corporation went out of business.

Hiller, in contrast, would indeed find long-term success in his dream of light helicopter production, although the sudden loss of Kaiser's financial backing late in 1945 might have seemed to suggest otherwise. What was left from this association—plus a $50,000 line of credit with Bank of America, which knew Hiller from his earlier successes—bought critical time during which he reformed Hiller Aircraft to continue rotary-wing development under the new name of United Helicopters.

Of approximately eighteen employees—a high point under Kaiser—half that number now remained to face an uncertain future. However great the challenges, this dedicated crew had strong faith in its young leader and the company he had created.

The Between Years

With a revised version in hand of the plan presented earlier to Henry Kaiser, Stanley Hiller, Jr., began courting the East and West Coast financial communities in quest of a million dollars in development funds. Investment banks and other conventional sources of capital were of no help, these institutions noting cautiously that the major aircraft manufacturers were for the most part ignoring helicopter development. The financial analysts wondered what these corporations knew about helicopters that made them shy away. They also wondered why Stanley Hiller and the renowned Henry Kaiser had chosen to end their mutual association: had the latter decided that helicopter production—obviously a questionable business venture—was simply fraught with too much risk?

It was indeed hard to argue that 1946 was the time to jump into helicopter production. Hiller persevered, nevertheless, eventually locating a small securities firm right in his own backyard willing to grant start-up monies even though it had yet to back a successful company. Capital Securities of Oakland, California, in fact subscribed more than $900,000 over four months to United Helicopters. United Helicopters also raised funds directly through continuing imaginative promotion of its products; a fact of life, these efforts were critical to staying in business.

Having moved into an old warehouse in Oakland in the fall of 1945, the company returned briefly to the Berkeley Armory, where it remained until May 1946, when it moved into the old Federal Telegraph Building in Palo Alto, directly across the street from the entrance to Stanford University. In the meantime, two new lines of helicopter development had begun.

The first was the company's first single-rotor helicopter, an open-frame single-seater called the J-5. Known informally as the "jet-torque helicopter," the novel craft countered torque by means of air ducted through a narrowing tail cone, thereby eliminating the need for a tail rotor. Not having a tail rotor was a worthwhile goal: besides siphoning off engine power and generating drag in forward flight, tail rotors were giving the young helicopter industry fits because of often-tragic failures of their wooden blades and long transmission shafts.

Designed as a testbed rather than a production prototype, the J-5 had a single main rotor thirty-two feet in diameter. Although it incorporated cyclic control, this rotor entirely lacked collective control. Its laminated wood blades—designed and built at Hiller—were fixed in pitch so that throttle alone determined the amount of lift generated (limiting the craft's efficiency much as a single gear ratio limits that of a bicycle). Despite the lack of pitch control, the J-5 could safely be autorotated in the event of an engine failure by diving and flaring at the right time. A vertically mounted 90-hp Franklin engine supplied power.

Starting in the fall of 1945, Ed Bennett built the J-5 from scratch except for its rotor blades. In his late thirties, well liked and capable, Bennett improvised as he went with only occasional questions for the engineering staff. By sparing the company the laborious process of working up detailed design drawings, he had the J-5 ready for testing in the University of California Memorial Stadium in March 1946. Bennett himself performed the first tethered flights in this machine.

The J-5 featured an engine-driven ducted fan that moved air aft through a tapering plenum. Most of this air was exhausted to the right to offset torque, but an adjustable outlet on the other side permitted proportionately more or less air to be ducted to the left to rotate the aircraft as desired about the yaw axis.

Company hopes for the jet-torque concept were high because it promised a cleaner, less complex machine. Better still, the single-main-rotor-with-no-tail-rotor configuration was one nobody else had used, and having a unique helicopter was a strong plus on the business front, where product differentiation is a powerful marketing tool.

Page Mill Road, a dirt road in a remote stretch of Stanford University's vast landholdings, was the site of flight tests commencing in late spring 1946.[1] Concrete pads—all that remained of temporary wartime buildings—provided debris-free aprons for the exhaustive evaluations. Tests validated the general concept but were otherwise disappointing. The J-5's yaw control response was unacceptably slow, primarily because of engine power limitations. The stability of the machine also left much to be desired, not surprising as the J-5 lacked any stabilizing mechanism.

Simply stated, the J-5 was ahead of its time; the state of the art in power plant technology was not advanced enough in 1946 to warrant intensive development of the no-tail-rotor concept. Igor Sikorsky and Frank Piasecki (unbeknownst to Hiller) had each considered this approach and rejected it without building prototypes; to Hiller, therefore, fell the distinction of building the first such machine.

A two-seat follow-on called the J-10 was designed but was abandoned before construction had progressed very far. Two more single-rotor, single-seat prototypes were the next to fly. Both featured conventional tail rotors and collective pitch, and both were known variously as UH-5s (denoting United Helicopters' fifth design) or NC-5s (this prefix humorously denoting "no control" because the design initially did not incorporate any mechanism for stability). The NC-5 designation would later also be applied retroactively to the J-5.

The second line of development began late in the fall of 1945 with a U.S. Navy industrywide request for proposals for development of a ship-based light

*H*iller hovers the single-rotor J-5 in
the spring of 1946. Development of the
no-tail-rotor helicopter concept was soon
shelved because of insufficient engine
power.

transport helicopter. The Hiller team responded in its first-ever bid to develop an entire military aircraft with a 450-hp five-place coaxial helicopter called the HO-346. Failing to win this contract, United Helicopters made this effort the basis of a design for a much smaller two-place personal machine.

The result was the UH-4 Commuter, an aluminum and Plexiglas teardrop of remarkable simplicity and startling beauty. As its name implied, it was intended strictly for private use. However novel the idea of home-based flying machines might seem today, it enjoyed wide acceptance at the time the Commuter came into being.

Automobiles having so profoundly altered society, America had come during the 1930s to expect aircraft to work similar changes in everyday life. Witnessing aviation's exuberant adolescence, a Depression-ridden United States embraced flight—humanity's oldest dream and a strong metaphor for freedom—as proof positive of better times to come. The vision of personal flying machines—inevitably the helicopter—and of aerial traffic speedily bypassing urban congestion at ground level was universally hailed.

The Wright brothers invented the airplane in 1903, Charles Lindbergh made jazz-age Americans "air minded" in 1927, and now World War II—in which aviation played a starring role—had taught hundreds of thousands of young Americans to fly. The United States, moreover, emerged from this global conflict all-powerful, its technological prowess matched only by the phenomenal productivity of its factories. All the elements seemed to be in place for realization of the then-popular dream of an aircraft in every garage.

"We all truly believed that," Stanley Hiller recalls. "I remember listening to Igor Sikorsky in some of his speeches talking about helicopters in every backyard. We believed it; that's why we sized and shaped the Commuters as a personal device."[2] So did fixed-wing aircraft manufacturers who brought to market personal machines, some (like the Erco Europe and the General Skyfarer) designed without rudder pedals, to make them easier to "drive." Nevertheless, the boom inexorably went bust by mid-1947, a catastrophic year for "general aviation," the broad term encompassing all nonmilitary and nonairline flying. For the time being, it seemed, flying machines would stay at the airport rather than come home.

The Commuter's specifications called for a cruise speed of 90–100 miles per hour, a range of 150 miles, and a rate of climb of 500 feet per minute. Its cabin, large enough to accommodate two people seated side by side as well as their suitcases, offered phenomenal visibility. A horizontally mounted 125-hp Lycoming drove its counterrotating teetering rotors through a two-stage five-gear transmission incorporating a mercury clutch for automatic engagement of the rotor upon starting.

Considerably refined over the company's earlier efforts, the Hiller UH-4 Commuter's all-metal rotor blades tapered in both thickness and planform. Two versions of this blade were constructed. The first was built around a hollow, tapered tube running from root to tip. The second employed a heavy

*T*he first Hiller UH-4 Commuter takes flight in July 1946. Hiller takes shop superintendent Smith Pettit aloft late on the day of the first flight. Courtesy NASM/SI.

*A*n uncontrollable lateral oscillation throws the UH-4 Commuter into a steep bank from which recovery is impossible. Fortunately, no one is hurt in the ensuing crash.

*P*iled wreckage underscores a lucky escape. Despite appearances, the prototype was quickly rebuilt and back in the air later that summer.

mandrel extending a third of the way out from the root, onto which aluminum stringers continuing the length of the blade were bonded. The entire airfoil assembly was then covered with riveted aluminum skin with magnesium trailing edges.

This latter unit, the last of five metal blade-types built by Hiller, was the first blade in the industry to rely on chemical bonding—in effect, gluing. Unique at the time of Hiller's pioneering efforts, rigid and bonded metal rotor blades would be adopted industrywide decades later.

The first UH-4 Commuter was already undergoing final assembly at the time of the move to temporary quarters in Palo Alto. Minus its cabin enclosure, this aircraft began ground testing at a site provided by Stanford University. It flew for the first time one bright morning in July 1946. Because its pilot was by now an old hand at flying coaxial helicopters, Stanley Hiller dispensed with restraining cables.

Toward the end of a long first day of testing, the open-frame Commuter was being evaluated in a nose-heavy condition with shop superintendent Smith D. Pettit accompanying Hiller as observer. Because the control stick stop was round, Hiller found that he could not move the stick left or right at its full-aft position. Unable, therefore, to counter a rapid side-to-side oscillation that developed, he was powerless to prevent the experimental prototype from slamming sideways into the ground.

Fortunately, neither the UH-4's occupants nor any ground personnel were seriously injured. This helicopter—the company's fifth to fly—looked worse

than it actually was, for the blades had absorbed much of the impact. It was quickly rebuilt with a squared stick stop, and testing was resumed later that summer. It was joined by UH-4 no. 2 late in 1946 and UH-4 no. 3 the following spring. In contrast to the first example, these later machines featured fully enclosed cabins.

Interestingly, Hiller's auditory perception of the crash of his Commuter was one of utter silence. Life-threatening incidents in the XH-44 had also seemed "silent," and none had left any noticeable aftereffects. "I really had no reaction," Hiller states. "It was something that had to be done."[3] In contrast, for Carolyn Hiller, who witnessed the UH-4 crash close at hand, the sights and sounds would remain with her. But likewise, when she and her husband together experienced a heartstoppingly close call in a light helicopter, she would shrug the incident off without a moment's notice.

With money from new financing now flowing in, Hiller traveled around the United States to talk with people involved in the rotary-wing industry. "You couldn't wait for people to come to you," he explained later. "You had to go to where you heard there were good people."[4]

One of the company president's first stops was the Kellett Autogyro Company of Upper Darby, Pennsylvania. Although the company was a well-known manufacturer of autogyros, it was in marked decline despite government sponsorship of several developments. Hiller found a number of engineers there who were keenly interested in his work. All expressed amazement at how much Hiller's West Coast group had accomplished in relative isolation and without government support.

First to leave Kellett and join United Helicopters was Wayne Wiesner, a soft-spoken expert in rotary-wing flight who replaced Harold Sigler as chief engineer. Sigler became overall head of engineering with troubleshooting duties more to his liking than the day-to-day engineering, which was Wiesner's strong suit. Wiesner's initial duties were in the area of structural engineering; his activities brought peace of mind to Hiller, who realized his operation had been skating on thin ice for some time because of rotor blade loads and other potentially hazardous phenomena not fully understood before.

Other Kellett personnel joining Hiller in the fall of 1946 were top dynamics/structural engineer Robert Wagner, design/weights engineer James Rigby, and noted structural/design engineer Webb Scheutzow. From Sikorsky came engineer Harold E. ("Hal") Lemont, Jr., who had participated in the closing stages of Igor Sikorsky's VS-300 program. Joe Stuart III, Robert Hurda, Dick Carlson, Don Jacoby, and Robert Anderson were a few more of the new faces at Hiller who would later be honored for their significant contributions to vertical-flight technology. One much later arrival of note would be Dr. J. A. J. Bennett (no relation to Edward Bennett), who would come all the way from England, where he was a towering figure in that country's rotary-wing development.

On the suggestion of United Helicopters board member Francis Callery, Hiller

also hired Frank Coffyn, who was then working for Liquidometer, an instrument company in the East. The last surviving member of the Wright brothers' original demonstration team, Coffyn was also the third licensed civil helicopter pilot in the United States. Tall, handsome, charismatic, married many times—nobody at Hiller knew for certain how many—the elderly "early bird" divided his time between promotional and research duties, taking frequent breaks to regale those around him with fascinating stories about the Wrights and flying's earliest days.

Also in 1946, a professional test pilot arrived to free Hiller for the full-time demands of running a growing company. Although at twenty-two scarcely older than his boss, Frank W. ("Pete") Peterson was nevertheless uniquely qualified. When World War II interrupted his electrical engineering studies at Texas A&M University, he volunteered for flight training with the Army Air Forces, and by 1943 he was test-flying fighters, bombers, trainers, and even captured enemy machines at Wright Field in Ohio. While there, he learned to fly helicopters under Colonel Frank Gregory and was assigned as service test pilot for the Sikorsky R-4. By war's end, Peterson had amassed hundreds of hours of helicopter time. Coincidentally, it was Frank Peterson who had taught Frank Coffyn to fly a helicopter.

The infusion of so much new talent added tremendous vigor to an already exciting environment. Fresh, dynamic, yet small enough to grant tremendous responsibility to those willing to shoulder it, United Helicopters soon built a

A newly manufactured UH-4 graces the parking lot of United Helicopters' temporary Palo Alto home. Hiller operated under this interim name from 1946 to 1951.

reputation that drew top people. The opportunity to work on rotary-wing flight, plus enviable living conditions in the Santa Clara Valley, were strong inducements to East Coast engineers to come West. Being the only rotary-wing company on the West Coast also gave Hiller his choice of graduates of Stanford University and California Polytechnic who wanted more out of a job than a desk amid a sea of others, as offered by the state's fixed-wing aircraft companies.

Hiller himself deliberately created the environment his stellar staff found so stimulating and so conducive to creative effort. He learned to match people to jobs, assigning projects in such a way that employees would adopt them as their own. Tasks formulated by Hiller, moreover, offered *real* challenges and satisfactions, not the formalized frustrations and limited pleasures offered by so many other companies. Hiller's philosophy of letting people know they were pursuing their own ideas and bringing to fruition their own projects paid huge dividends in morale and productivity.

The top man always sets the tone. The tone Hiller set was one of honorable dealings with others, respectful attention to those around him, and extremely hard work in pursuit of a shared vision of vertical flight. It was this tantalizing vision that made the struggling Hiller company an exciting place to work.

The United Helicopters UH-4 Commuter helicopter was publicly unveiled at the San Francisco Presidio on 18 March 1947 before a large crowd that included Army officers, civic leaders, and West Coast businessmen. There the trim craft demonstrated precision takeoffs and land-ings and a variety of other maneuvers. Particularly impressive was its ability to leap into the air, rotate on its vertical axis, and skim off in any direction while climbing and accelerating.

For building the world's first successful two-place coaxial helicopter, United Helicopters received top honors at the World Inventors Exposition in Los Angeles in July 1947, winning over Preston Tucker and his Tucker Torpedo automobile, which came in second. By this time, however, Hiller had given up any plans for production of the Commuter. It was a difficult decision—the trim UH-4 was a personal favorite—but it was now evident that the age of personal helicopters was simply not at hand, nor even around the corner. Instead, United Helicopters announced its decision to proceed with a versatile working helicopter intended for commercial and agricultural use.

A fundamental breakthrough in helicopter control had by now considerably brightened prospects for such a machine. Pilot Frank Peterson had established that the hovering stability of the first two NC-5s (the J-5 and its conventional successor) left much to be desired. Although equipped with collective pitch and a tail rotor, NC-5 no. 2 (also called UH-5A) proved tricky and overly sensitive, particularly in the roll axis. The lack of stability was demonstrated when the machine, which flew in the fall of 1946, crashed while hovering at Palo Alto Airport. Despite Peterson's best efforts, it turned over and, with a buzz-saw clatter, the rotor blades whittled themselves down to a fraction of their original length.

The dejected test pilot perched on the wreckage while others began collecting

*E*legant and simple, the UH-4 was designed for a widely anticipated age of personal flight which failed to dawn after World War II. This publicity photo reveals the Commuter's intended role as aerial automobile.

pieces. Hiller and other members of the team gathered around what moments before had been a flyable helicopter. An earnest discussion ensued as a solution was sought to the crippling stability problem. Having heard of the airfoil "paddles" Hiller had drawn in 1940 as a means of aerodynamically boosting the main rotor controls, engineer Joe Stuart interjected this concept into the conversation. Instant excitement dispelled the gloom, and as is often the case with discovery, the solution fell into place surprisingly quickly; in perhaps a minute and a half, a totally new and truly revolutionary control system had been conceived.

The answer was an aerodynamic cyclic control consisting of airfoil-shaped paddles mounted on the rotor head at right angles to the blades. With this fundamentally new approach to helicopter control and stabilization, the pilot does not have to "twist" the heavy rotor system directly;[5] instead, his cyclic stick controls the paddles, which in turn adjust the main rotor. The new system promised positive dynamic stability, light control forces, and freedom from the fatiguing vibration passed down other helicopters' control sticks.

Ed Bennett worked all that night and by morning he had an aerodynamic cyclic control flying in the quarter-scale on one of his experimental shop's electrically powered models. This model showed astounding stability. Excitement remained high as Bennett set about rebuilding the J-5 into a testbed for what was christened the Hiller "Rotormatic" cyclic control. The craft was ready for testing in short order.

Flown in the spring of 1947, the NC-5 no. 3 (UH-5B) was far more stable than any helicopter flown up to that time. Peterson, in fact, found the trim single-seater *too* stable, a complaint easily addressed by increasing the size and decreasing the weight of the paddles. In a no-wind situation, the UH-5B could be lifted from the ground, hovered for an extended period of time, and landed again without the pilot having to touch the overhead cyclic stick. Such a feat was unthinkable in a Bell or a Sikorsky. To illustrate this unprecedented stability, the company released photographs of the craft hovering with only piled sandbags in the pilot's seat.

Today all but forgotten, the UH-5B is profoundly significant as the first truly stable helicopter. The dynamics of helicopter flight are such that helicopters are inherently *un*stable, a lesson learned by most early pioneers. In order to make a successful helicopter, therefore, some mechanism to introduce stability is usually required.[6]

Most early helicopter manufacturers failed to address this problem adequately, if at all, thereby consigning many rotary-wing pilots to constant fatiguing corrections and occasional mishaps. The first Sikorskys were notorious in this regard. Arthur M. Young, designer of the famous Bell 47, achieved stability with some compromise to control response with his patented "fly bar," a counterweighted shaft set at right angles to the rotor blades. Hiller's aerodynamic approach went further still, for unlike Bell's fly bar it required no compromise between controllability and stability.

In a dramatic demonstration of the

In a dramatic demonstration of positive dynamic stability, Ed Bennett shoves the tire of the NC-5 as Frank Peterson, Hiller's first professional test pilot, holds his hands away from the controls. Within three quickly diminishing oscillations, the helicopter would return itself to a motionless hover.

UH-5Bs capabilities, Peterson would hover several feet off the ground with his hands outstretched to show he was not touching the controls. Bennett would then approach, grasp the tire of the little machine, and give it a violent shove to induce a wild pendular swing. Witnessing the demonstration, *Aviation Week* editor Scholer Bangs noted with amazement that "within three quickly diminishing oscillations the 'copter restores to its hovering attitude."[7]

The strong character of this unusual group of helicopter developers impressed Bangs. "Hiller and his group individually work prodigious hours," he observed, "and with zealot enthusiasm shed titles to become errand boys and janitors when indicated. [Treasurer] Henry L. McIntyre . . . and Langhorne Washburn, operations manager, told this writer separately that U.H. spirit is such that no work is contracted outside the organization if the job—no matter how small or large—possibly can be done by a company worker or executive during or after regular working hours."[8]

About this time, Frank Peterson took time off from flight-test duties to get married. Not long after he and the new Mrs. Peterson set off on a honeymoon camping trip along California's Russian River, a unique opportunity arose for Hiller to demonstrate the UH-5B to giant Convair in San Diego. Unfortunately, United Helicopters was given only one day's notice. The helicopter with support crew was hurriedly dispatched by truck to drive south all night, and official help was meanwhile enlisted to locate the Petersons. Within hours, the stunned newlyweds were roused from their

appreciation of nature and each other by the California Highway Patrol. "We got him on an airplane and sent him all the way down to San Diego," Hiller recalls with a smile, "and he made a nice demonstration the next morning, his wife absolutely enraged."[9]

On another occasion, aviation reporter William Flynn and photographer Bob Campbell of the *San Francisco Chronicle* visited Palo Alto to see the stable helicopter they had heard so much about. Stanley Hiller greeted them cordially in his office. "Have you ever flown a plane?" Hiller inquired of Campbell. The photographer admitted that he had not. "Fine," the company president replied. Ground school concluded, Hiller led them to the "flying field"—a small parking area perhaps big enough for thirty cars—just outside the door. A light wind was blowing as mechanic Tex Swanson started the UH-5B's engine, warming it as the rotors swished over his head. Campbell, a veteran of Iwo Jima, gulped and let himself be strapped into the single seat at the front of the open framework. He listened as the controls were explained to him: stick over his right shoulder, rudder bar under his feet, and throttle and collective pitch levers below his left hand.

With Swanson standing by the aft fuselage and Peterson to Campbell's right, Hiller took up his station at the photographer's left to give instructions. Under his tutelage, the novice pilot levitated the craft into the air. Hiller dismissed his subordinates early on and then himself walked away after just sixteen minutes, leaving Campbell successfully compensating for the wind while maintaining position above the ground. Because hovering a helicopter is demanding at the best of times, Flynn's article might well have been disbelieved had it found its way to the Bell and Sikorsky plants back East.[10]

Before committing his company to producing a single-rotor helicopter, Hiller reconfigured the first UH-4 Commuter with three aerodynamic paddles between its coaxial rotor heads. Although the modification produced an instant improvement in stability, it also made for an unwieldy and overly complex rotor assembly. United Helicopters' first production helicopter, therefore, would have just one main rotor and a tail rotor.

This decision presented a major problem of its own. Having obtained financing by selling investors on the idea of the new and different coaxial configuration, Hiller was now faced with the task of undoing what had been done and then gaining investors' support for a more conventional machine. Wisely, he invited them to make up their own minds at the Redwood City High School football field. Some four thousand investors watched the UH-4 Commuter and UH-5B being put through their paces while their relative advantages and disadvantages were discussed. When the demonstration ended, Hiller had virtually unanimous support for the single-main-rotor-with-tail-rotor approach.

Eight helicopters in fourteen different configurations had been tested over almost four years to arrive at this juncture. No other manufacturer could begin to demonstrate such a lineup of experimental prototypes giving expression to so much creativity and variety. With a production configuration at last selected and development of a new prototype under way, in 1947 Hiller purchased a 61-acre tract of land on the outskirts of Palo Alto and set about building a long-needed permanent base of operations. All the elements were finally in place to realize the long-held dream of production.

Willow Road

On the heels of the dramatic success of UH-5B, United Helicopters initiated development early in 1947 of a production prototype designated the Hiller 360 (also called the Model UH-12 when introduced late in 1948 and later simply the Model 12). The Hiller 360's sterling qualities in civil and military service would keep it in production for almost four decades, making it the longest-produced helicopter in the industry.

The new Hiller 360 was unique in that it was the product of an organization formed specifically to build civil helicopters. In contrast, Bell and Sikorsky—the only other manufacturers successfully addressing the civil helicopter market in the 1940s—were established fixed-wing aircraft companies.

The Hiller 360, moreover, would be the first helicopter to achieve full production without any direct or indirect military funding. Sikorsky's R-4 and Piasecki's HRP-1 were strictly military ventures. Bell's Model 47 was a civil aircraft, of course, but it had been nurtured with profits from Bell's lucrative wartime military aircraft production. In view of the enormous technological difficulties presented by the challenge and the limited profits to be made from its realization, Hiller's success with a privately financed helicopter is truly remarkable.

In its first years in production, Hiller sold more civil helicopters than did all the other companies combined. As impressive as this statement might sound, there were really only three other companies in the world engaged in volume helicopter production before the outbreak of the Korean War. Of these, only Bell Aircraft provided Hiller with meaningful competition, since Sikorsky and Piasecki concentrated on military production. The few Sikorsky S-51s sold commercially were big enough not to detract from Hiller's or Bell's sales, whereas the ungainly S-52 two-seater was a commercial flop. The first flight of Sikorsky's eight- to ten-place S-55 in late 1949, moreover, signaled that company's intention to manufacture big helicopters rather than little ones.

Piasecki Helicopter Corporation of Philadelphia had already beaten Sikorsky to the emerging market for large military helicopters. Formed by engineer Frank N. Piasecki, who flew America's second successful helicopter in April 1943, in February 1944 this company received a Navy contract calling for development of a large helicopter. Thirteen months later, the banana-shaped Piasecki XHRP-X *Dogship* made its first flight, and the first production HRP-1 was delivered to the Navy in November 1947. The *Dogship* was the world's first successful tandem-rotor helicopter and is the ancestor of the familiar Boeing H-47 Chinook transport helicopters of today.[1]

With Bell and Hiller competing in small helicopters and Sikorsky and Piasecki focusing on large machines, helicopter manufacture was coalescing by the end of the seminal 1940s into a well-balanced industry. Other successful companies would establish themselves, of course; one was already building helicopters, although it would not achieve volume production before 1950. Kaman (pronounced Kuh-MAN) Helicopters, located at Bradley Field near Hartford, Connecticut, would successfully address an as-yet-untapped market for intermediate-size military machines.

Bell was the second company in the United States to set up an assembly line. Certified in May 1946, its familiar Model 47—the first production-line *civil* helicopter—grew directly out of pioneering research initiated by Pennsylvanian Arthur M. Young in the late 1920s. A philosopher and inventor, Young pursued a pragmatic step-by-step study of helicopter flight with electrically powered models he built by hand. Young's success—notably in developing the stabilizing bar that would adorn the rotors of Bell helicopters for years to come—led Lawrence D. Bell to bring him to Buffalo in 1941.

Arthur Young, Bartram Kelley, and the rest of Bell's small helicopter team soon set up shop in a disused automobile dealership in Gardenville, New York. With car manufacture halted for the war effort, the facility had been closed for the duration. There the first Bell helicopter—a single-seater designated the Model 30—made its initial free flight late in June 1943. It and two other preproduction prototypes were followed by the historic Model 47, which to the American public would soon become *the* light helicopter, just as Bill Piper's J-3 Cub was *the* light airplane.

Hiller's newer machine was similar overall to Bell's. Both featured the single-main-rotor-with-small-vertical-tail-rotor configuration perfected by (but not invented by) Igor Sikorsky on his VS-300. These production light helicopters were both powered by the same engine, weighed approximately the same, featured similar dimensions, and—not surprisingly—offered roughly comparable performance.[2] Both would evolve over time through successively better—and still fairly comparable—models.

From a product-support standpoint, early helicopter operators preferred dealing with a well-established and experienced outfit like the Bell company, which from the outset gave top priority to customer satisfaction.[3] Despite heroic efforts, Hiller had insufficient resources and experience to match Bell in this department until after the Korean War.

From a technological standpoint, however, the new Hiller 360 was superior to the Bell Model 47. It was so stable that it could be trimmed for extended "hands-off" cruise, whereas the Bell—the next most stable helicopter then in existence—could not be flown for more than a few seconds with hands off the control stick. The Hiller 360, moreover, featured all-metal semimonocoque construction, needed less maintenance, boasted a greater useful load, and cost less to purchase and operate.

Nevertheless, United Helicopters would learn that building a "better mousetrap" did not in itself guarantee success over time. Bell, in fact, had three advantages that would always keep it a formidable competitor and that by the latter 1950s would tip the scales inexorably in its favor. First, the Model 47 benefited from the parent company's fame as an established military contractor, a reputation further enhanced when Air Force Captain Charles E. ("Chuck") Yeager shattered the sound barrier on 14 October 1947 in his bullet-shaped Bell X-1 rocket plane.

Second, although Bell Aircraft in the immediate postwar era (even more than most wartime manufacturers) was reduced to a mere shadow of its former self, it could nevertheless support helicopter development far more lavishly than could privately financed Hiller.[4] Its wartime production of fighter planes, armament systems, and (under license at an Army-owned factory in Marietta, Georgia) B-29 bombers had left the Bell company with vast financial reserves.

Third, Bell had an insider's understanding of procurement, that complex process whereby the military services purchase aircraft. As a newcomer, Hiller did not; much time would be lost and many mistakes made as the company struggled to learn how to secure and retain military business.

Certainly military business played (as it does to this day) a preemptive role in shaping the rotary-wing industry. Being substantially more complex than fixed-wing airplanes of comparable weight and power, helicopters cost more to build, operate, and maintain; as a result, they enjoy commercial success only in those areas where their unique abilities are required. Such being the case, it is scarcely surprising that commercial sales alone have traditionally represented too small a production base to guarantee enduring financial health to any helicopter manufacturer.

With limited markets, it is hardly surprising that rivalry between Bell and Hiller would grow intense. Hiller people called the Model 47 the "Belly-Copter" (after Bell's own brief use of the unfortunate term "Bellicopter" during World War II) or "Brand X," pointedly ignoring the fact that Bell had beat Hiller to the marketplace by fully two years. Bell salesmen, in turn, found it an effective tactic to allude darkly to the "Hiller killer" to sway undecided customers in favor of their product.

The industry was then so small that one generally knew one's counterparts in the other camp, and relations at common gatherings ranged from civil to very friendly. But behind the scenes in both companies was the constant struggle to provide more for less, to improve upon the other's product, and otherwise to outdo one's rival. Such competition kept both companies fit and trim while guaranteeing customers maximum value for their money.

By way of example, in September 1948 Bell Aircraft raised its price for the Model 47D utility helicopter from $25,000 to

$39,500. President Larry Bell attributed the sharp increase to the high cost of developing accessory equipment such as dusting and spraying gear for aerial application. "We have had to go even further," he lamented, "spending large sums proving the helicopter's superiority in pest control over many types of . . . crops."[5] Just a month later, the Hiller 360 received civil certification and became available to the public at $19,995. Its monopoly suddenly gone, Bell dropped its price back down to $23,500. Bell had not been greedy; its price hike had reflected genuine costs. By the time commercial deliveries of the Model 47 commenced in December 1946, in fact, already more than a million work-hours of engineering and labor, 4,000 hours of experimental flight testing, and nearly $5 million had gone into the Model 47.[6] Getting to market, it turned out, was just the beginning, for nobody really knew what to do with a helicopter. Before long, Bell found itself developing a vast array of agricultural and other gear which it demonstrated on its helicopters both in the United States and abroad, all at its own cost, in the hope of generating business.

In short, Bell had found (as would Hiller to a lesser degree) that introducing any new technology is an expensive proposition.[7] The cost of educating potential customers as to what the helicopter could do for them had forced the New York company to reach deeper into its corporate pockets than it had ever intended. With a monopoly came the opportunity to recoup fairly quickly; with competition from United Helicopters in California, however, Bell Aircraft was forced to forgo a quick return to maintain market share and stay in production.

The value of free-market competition could not have been more eloquently demonstrated. Competition also paid dividends when the U.S. Government was the customer. "Bell and Hiller kept developing new machines to bid against each other at their own cost," stated former Hiller military contracts manager William D. Rollnick. "The Army bought them finally, but the incentive was always to keep increasing the performance and making it a better machine."[8]

An interesting footnote to the rivalry was the role of Larry Bell himself. A visionary who (alone among the top management of his fixed-wing aircraft company) believed in the future of rotary-wing flight, Bell permitted Stan Hiller to share Bell's source for rotor blades so that the Californian could get into production with his rival 360. A few years later, Bell turned over to the Army some of Bell Aircraft's stockpile of 500 Franklin 178-hp helicopter engines so that Hiller could fulfill rush Army orders for Hiller evacuation helicopters during the Korean War. Larry Bell helped partly because he believed the emerging market to be large enough to support another light helicopter manufacturer, and partly because his long career in aviation had taught him the value of healthy competition.

Prospects clearly looked bright for United Helicopters as development of the new 360 progressed. Studying a full-size mock-up of their new rotorcraft, the Hiller team realized immediately that a conventional two-seat arrangement was undesirable. Because the pilot always fills one seat, a two-place machine is, from a commercial perspective, only a single-seater. Room for *two* passengers plus pilot, Hiller and his group saw, offered vastly more utility with minimum added expense.

Two-person mountain survey teams, executives conferring en route to meetings—the list of possible charter opportunities that would be lost to operators of two-seat helicopters was a long one. The Hiller 360 was therefore redesigned to be a three-place machine before the production prototype ever flew. Bell, whose Model 47 had two seats, copied this three-place feature on the 47D-1.

As it went together, the prototype Hiller 360 simply looked *right*. Poised on its tricycle landing gear like some elegant piece of technological sculpture, it gleamed from the nose of its low-slung silver fuselage to the tip of its rakish tail. The shine came from stressed-skin construction like that of modern airliners. In contrast, the Bell 47's welded steel-tube structure harkened back to the era of fabric-covered airplanes like the Piper Cub.

The single retrograde step in the 360's design, in fact, was the use of wooden blades on its teetering rotor. Engineers Arthur Young and Charles Seibel, both helicopter pioneers of the first rank, had developed these blades for use on the Bell Model 47. Made of laminated spruce with laminated balsa trailing edges, reinforced internally with stainless steel straps anchored by retaining pins at the hub, these blades were covered in fiberglass and their leading edges were further protected with stainless steel.

Continuing the tradition established

by Hiller's earlier coaxial machines, the Hiller 360 was to have had metal rotor blades. The Universal Helicopter Corporation of Buffalo, New York, a company formed in 1946 expressly to manufacture blades for rotorcraft builders, developed metal blades under contract to Hiller, but at the eleventh hour these units proved not to be fatigue-resistant. With production imminent and no time to develop new blades from scratch, Hiller—as reported above—turned to Larry Bell. Bell agreed to let the Palo Alto group purchase Bell-type blades from Bell Aircraft's supplier, the Parsons Corporation's Aircraft Division at Traverse City, Michigan.

Eight years later, with the introduction of the H-23D in 1957, the company would finally return to the all-metal rotor blades it had pioneered. The Hiller 360's tail rotor was all-metal from the start, a substantial improvement over Bell's wooden tail rotor, which frequently suffered damage from stones kicked up by main rotor downwash.

The new 360 employed other innovations in addition to the Rotormatic cyclic. One was the use of tension-torsion bars—first used on Kellett Autogyros in the early 1940s—to connect the main rotor blades to the hub. Made up of forty-three parallel pieces of steel, these laminates simultaneously held the blades to the hub yet twisted to allow them to change pitch. This ingenious system reduced weight and complexity by dispensing with the thrust bearings used in other helicopters. These bars would prove reliable and maintenance-free over the decades to come.

Efforts to reduce construction time,

save weight, improve accessibility, and minimize maintenance requirements were evident throughout the Hiller 360. The housing of its mercury clutch and other parts were designed to reduce production time. The power train was streamlined by designing the rotor head, transmission, and vertically mounted 160-hp Aircooled Motors (Franklin) engine into one integral unit that could be lifted out by removing just six bolts at the rubber Lord mounts, which effectively isolated the rest of the aircraft from engine and rotor vibration during flight.

The transmission itself was simple, although it would suffer some "teething troubles." In contrast to the Bell 47's two-stage transmission employing twenty-four gears, Hiller's single-stage unit provided a 9.17 to 1 reduction with just six gears.

Another new feature was the Hiller's overhead stick, which connected directly to the paddle linkages. Eliminating almost all the control pulleys, rods, and cams found in other helicopter control systems, the overhead stick enhanced safety because—in contrast to helicopters in which the main rotor-control linkages are buried in the airframe—one could verify visually during preflight inspection that everything was properly connected.

Finally, the Hiller 360 employed a bladder-type fuel cell buried in its fuselage pan under a protective stainless steel deck. More complex and costly than Bell-style gravity-fed external metal tanks, this system substantially enhanced safety. External fuel tanks were in fact a problem with the early Bells; in a crash, they could rip loose and smash through the Plexiglas cockpit bubble.

The Hiller 360X ("X" for experimental) took to the air on 11 November 1947, at 5:20 P.M., in a flight that brought no surprises thanks to some 150 hours of exhaustive testing flown by Peterson in the UH-5B. The new prototype's cabin was fully enclosed like that of an automobile, reflecting a persistent though unwarranted belief in the personal helicopter market. Its color and ungainly lines—one employee likened it to "a yellow overstuffed dragonfly"—earned it the unflattering nickname *Yellow Peril*.[9] This machine was demonstrated to the U.S. Army and Navy before being unveiled to the public on 11 December 1947.

Hiller's new helicopter quickly became the focus of media attention, in part because its announced price of under $20,000—lower than that of other helicopters—promised to hasten acceptance of light commercial helicopters. Tests confirmed a top speed of 85 mph with an endurance of 2.5 hours and a range of 212 miles. Vertical rate of climb was 400 feet per minute, and maximum initial climb with forward airspeed was almost 1000 fpm. Service ceiling was 12,000 feet. With an empty weight of 1,453 pounds and a gross weight of 2,200 pounds, the useful load was a respectable 747 pounds—enough for a pilot and two passengers plus 60 pounds of baggage and 29 gallons of gasoline.

Published descriptions of the aircraft stressed unheard-of stability and controllability. Spring-balanced and self-centering in flight, the overhead stick required a mere 15-ounce fingertip pressure to produce the desired response. The centering springs also served to provide artificial control-feel, there being none in the literal sense because the pilot did not directly control the main rotor.

Because the rotors passed through 180 degrees of travel before paddle input was fully translated to the main rotor, a slight but unobtrusive control lag was perceptible. This lag actually served to screen out unintentional control inputs, including violent jolts. Although the 360X responded quickly to light, steady inputs, its stick could be moved suddenly in straight lines or through complete circles without any rotor reaction. In contrast to the few other helicopters in production, moreover, the new helicopter's stick transmitted no bothersome feedback forces from the main rotor.

Interestingly enough, where other manufacturers faced the gloomy prospect of heavier controls as they designed larger machines, Hiller Rotormatic forces were entirely a function of the size of the paddles and the mechanical advantage designed into their linkages; the paddles, in short, offered light forces regardless of the size of the helicopter. Boosted controls such as had been used in fixed-wing aircraft since World War II would be the route other manufacturers would take to address the problem of heavy controls, and the advent of stability-augmentation systems would eventually help them close the gap in stability. For some years to come, however, the Hiller 360 would continue to do things that helicopters built by other companies could not.

Skepticism among these other manufacturers was laid to rest at the Institute of Aeronautical Sciences Annual Meeting, convened in New York City at the start of 1948. During the rotary-wing session of 26 January 1948, Stanley Hiller

showed movies illustrating the unique characteristics of the Hiller 360, and Joe Stuart presented a technical paper titled "The Helicopter Rotor Control." Although their efforts did much to allay doubts about the effectiveness of the Rotormatic control, the relative value of this system in service remained a hotly debated issue.

Hiller moved his company into its brand new Palo Alto home at 1350 Willow Road on 3 April 1948. Stockholders attending the annual meeting were on hand for the dedication ceremonies, which included a performance by the 360X. An ideal site, the Willow Road property combined highway and rail-spur access (the latter never needed by Hiller) with verdant surroundings flat enough to permit light airplane operations. With a concrete apron at the rear of the factory serving as a flight line, the facility suggested an airport, although the unique capabilities of the helicopter rendered the construction of a runway unnecessary.

New aircraft types are required to run the gauntlet of government certification before they enter production. To speed up this difficult process, construction of three additional preproduction 360s was initiated before the move to Willow Road. The first of these new machines immediately disappeared under a massive static test frame in which it was stretched, twisted, and otherwise battered. It emerged six months later, the broken but nonetheless victorious winner of a Civil Aeronautics Administration (CAA) stamp of approval. The two other new prototypes joined the original 360 in flight trials.

In contrast to the 360X *Yellow Peril*,

*An aerial view shows the factory
at 1350 Willow Road, Palo Alto,
California. Hay grown on the property
was sold during the difficult early days.*

No other helicopter company in the world could demonstrate the variety of experimentation visible in this lineup on Hiller's flight ramp in 1948. Missing are the three X-2-235s, which were lost in Hiller's split from Kaiser, and the NC-5 no. 2, which crashed. The J-5 was rebuilt as the NC-5 no. 3 (third from left on ground).

these new machines had just a windscreen
to which a top panel and side doors
could be added for operation in incle-
ment weather. Having at last perceived
that his product would sell to commercial
operators rather than private owners for
whom a helicopter would be analogous
to a car, Hiller had dispensed with the
enclosed cabin. The uprated 178-hp
engine was also left uncovered, thereby
improving cooling and saving additional
weight.

On 14 October 1948, the CAA (predecessor of today's Federal Aviation
Administration) issued production certificate 6-H-1, denoting the first helicopter
to receive a certificate in the CAA's sixth
region. In a ceremony held at San Francisco's Marina District, where Hiller had
unveiled the XH-44 four years earlier, a
CAA representative painted "6-H-1" on
the hovering prototype, replacing the
word "Experimental."

Hiller thus became the third company
(after Bell and Sikorsky) to receive
approval to produce commercial helicopters. Significantly, in the course of
certification the CAA had determined
that the Hiller 360 possessed positive
dynamic stability, in contrast to the Bell
and Sikorsky machines, which—although
controllable—were not completely stable.

The bulbous 360X would continue in
test duties at Hiller into the 1950s. Upon
retirement, it was presented to the
Federal Aviation Administration for
classroom-training use, but the where-
abouts of this historic prototype is today
unknown.

Before certification of the Hiller
360, production contracts were let with
more than a hundred subcontractors

*C*ertification of the Hiller 360 on 14 October 1948—a company milestone— occasions a photograph of virtually the entire staff of United Helicopters except, ironically enough, the engineering department. Courtesy A. W. B. Vincent.

(almost all on the West Coast) who would initially build some 70 percent of the helicopter. Although certain parts were built at the Palo Alto factory, most of the work performed there was assembly and finishing rather than construction. Later, plant expansion and the acquisition of additional tooling would permit phasing out most of the subcontracting as a means of reducing production costs.

By the end of 1947, all thoughts of production looked decidedly premature to Hiller; funds raised earlier were running out just when badly needed manufacturing equipment and parts were drastically increasing the company's expenses. With capital still not available from conventional sources, Hiller turned again to Capital Securities only to find that the venture capital group was by now almost out of business.

Refusing to concede defeat so close to production, the Hiller team proposed to assist that ailing organization's securities sales force. Before this joint effort could gear up, however, several hundred thousand dollars of desperately needed bridge financing had to be found. In these very tough times, Hiller, company officers Henry McIntyre and A. W. B. ("Bill") Vincent, and board member Francis Callery together provided this money in a demonstration of faith in their new helicopter. Without it, the Hiller 360 would not have achieved production.

Already well-traveled at age twenty-seven, fellow investor Bill Vincent was the scion of a wealthy Irish family. A veteran of the British Army's long Burma campaign, he joined United Helicopters as a vice-president in January 1948. His knowledge of far-off places was valuable in developing a superb world-wide marketing strategy for the Hiller 360. Vincent would later direct all commercial sales, domestic and foreign. "We were all quite amateurs," Bill Vincent recalls today, "but the 360 was an exciting product and Stanley Hiller collected exciting people around him."[10]

Selling the 360 presented huge challenges. Most foreign countries had yet to see a helicopter and did not know what it could do. When it was explained to them, they often assumed that the Hiller machine could do far more than was possible for any first-generation helicopter. Lining up distributors to sell the 360 was also a problem. Bill Vincent remembers sitting in a cafe in Siam with a young Thai who had committed himself to marketing 360s. "Tell me," the man repeatedly implored Vincent. "How do I sell a helicopter? *How do I sell a helicopter?*"[11]

Englishman John Chadwick—who spent two and a half years flying RAF bombers during the war—joined Hiller in 1945 and oversaw certification of the 360. The first company vice-president, Chadwick would move to Europe in 1958 to take up international marketing duties assisting Bill Vincent.

Like Vincent, lawyer Henry McIntyre was independently wealthy and did not have to work for a living. McIntyre was the "old man" of the management team and opted for long hours as the company's secretary-treasurer. Another resourceful and dedicated Hiller employee was the operations officer C. Langhorne Washburn, an aviation-minded New Englander who had flown

In 1947, four thousand investors watch as a Commuter is put through its aerial paces at Redwood City's high school football field.

U.S. Navy patrol bombers during World War II. Hiller recognized in Washburn a natural public relations man whose talents would contribute much to the success of the Hiller 360.

Aware of the need for effective corporate governance, over the years Hiller sought top people to serve as directors of his public company. Typical of the caliber of the board members he recruited were Francis Callery, a former partner of a major Wall Street brokerage house, and I. M. Laddon, president of Consolidated-Vultee. Three former military men would also serve on the Hiller board: Dick Richardson, a retired admiral who later became vice-president for research and development at General Dynamics; Pierpont Morgan Hamilton, a retired U.S. Air Force brigadier general who learned to fly in 1917 and was awarded the Medal of Honor during World War II; and Frank Heileman, a retired U.S. Army major general whose last assignment had been as chief of the Army Transportation Corps. Officers-cum-investors Hiller, McIntyre, and Vincent were also members.

Frank Peterson soon had help on the flight line. Jay Demming, a superb former military flier, arrived in 1948 to take to the air as Hiller's second professional test pilot. Demming was the second of many very fine pilots employed in Hiller's flight test division, men like Fred Feinberg (after whom the helicopter industry's annual Feinberg Award is named), James Meade, Bruce Jones, Robert Boughton (who was also the number-two man in Hiller marketing), Phil Johnston, Dick Peck, and others.

Peterson and Demming early on shared what must rank as each man's most embarrassing moment with the company. While autorotating the Hiller 360X, confusion arose as to who was pilot in command. The test pilots were still wrestling over the controls when the prototype "crashed" with minor damage, injuring only their pride. Procedures were tightened up to avoid such incidents in the future. Meanwhile, the test pilots endured merciless kidding from their fellow Hiller employees, who perceived a measure of humor in the incident.

Visitors to that year's California State Fair were startled to see gleaming Hiller helicopters displayed between the usual milking machines and hay bailers. In the infield of a racetrack, these working machines gave convincing demonstrations of "air farming," a term invented by the company to describe such activities as dusting, spraying, and fruit drying. Similar active promotion throughout the state successfully accomplished three goals. First, it generated an awareness of the need for the company's new product. Second, it provided advance orders for production examples. Third, it sold a great deal of common stock. All told, more than $1.5 million in production financing was successfully raised.

An unusual flight early in 1949 dramatically focused national attention on the new helicopter. Widely published air-to-air photographs showed a Hiller 360 cruising at 2,500 feet over San Francisco Bay with nobody aboard; closer inspection revealed two goggled and parachuted figures clinging to its sides aft of the empty cockpit. The figures were Stan Hiller and Lang Washburn. With weights in the front to make it

*W*earing leather helmets, goggles, winter flying clothes, and parachutes, Stan Hiller and Lang Washburn cling to the sides of a Hiller 360 cruising high above San Francisco Bay in January 1949. No other helicopter then in existence could duplicate this feat.

nose-heavy, the Hiller 360 took off and climbed for altitude. As planned, Washburn then crawled far back along the fuselage pan while Hiller trimmed the craft to maintain level flight. Hiller then abandoned the cockpit and moved back along the other side of the helicopter while Washburn came partway forward again to maintain trim. There the men stayed while the 360 cruised serenely along from south of Moffett Field to San Carlos, a distance of a dozen miles. It could have flown on until its fuel was exhausted, but the point had been made; the Hiller 360 had extraordinary stability. No other helicopter in existence in 1949 could have flown this demonstration.

This remarkable flight drew its inspiration from another aerial demonstration made forty-five years earlier by aviator/inventor Lawrence B. Sperry. At the International Aeroplane Safety Contest in Bezons, France, on 18 June 1914, Sperry released the controls of his low-flying Curtiss flying boat and stood, hands raised high, while mechanic Emile Cachin climbed from the open cockpit to walk far out along the lower wing. He looked for all the world like a weight being slid to the end of a doctor's scale. To the amazement of onlookers below, the pilotless biplane did not tilt and crash. A Sperry autopilot—the first ever invented—had kept it level.

Hiller 360 production began early in 1949. The historic first commercial delivery took place on 1 March, when B. F. Hodges of Walnut Grove, California, accepted one of the preproduction 360s for dusting and spraying in the Sacramento Valley. Deliveries of assembly-line machines commenced in May. List price for the Hiller was $19,995, and the cost to dealers was just $16,000. This financial incentive of course prompted most early customers to proclaim themselves dealers, thereby building up United Helicopters' roster of distributorships.

If even $16,000 was more than the average private flier could afford to pay (by comparison, a new 1949 Beechcraft Bonanza four-seat airplane cost half as much), it was nevertheless substantially less than the cost of any other helicopter and well within reach of even modestly funded commercial operators. Orders for the 360 soon sustained a production rate of three per week, less than half the factory's maximum production rate of one per day.

Early in 1949, a preproduction 360 undertook America's first civil transcontinental helicopter flight.[12] The roundabout three-month tour—flown primarily by chief test pilot Frank Peterson—covered some 5,200 miles and included demonstrations at more than 450 centers across the United States. The helicopter took this arduous journey completely in stride as it lined up distributors, generated advance sales, and even performed a rescue along the way. Hiller himself—taking over in New Jersey to fly the last leg—piloted the gleaming machine into Manhattan and landed at the foot of Wall Street on 12 April.

Langhorne Washburn's promotional genius found brilliant expression in New York. "We wanted to show off the helicopter we had flown East," Stanley Hiller recalled by way of example, "and Lang said, 'Ah, I know what we'll do; we'll just take it apart and take it up the elevator of

The first civil helicopter to cross the United States lifts off on 24 January 1949. Palo Alto Mayor Walter Gaspar and Hiller bid farewell to employees Washburn, Peterson, and Rice as they begin a circuitous three-month 9,000-mile demonstration tour.

the Waldorf Astoria Hotel, where we'll put it back together.' Our crew did just that during the night, and the next morning this helicopter was there. Nobody knew how it had been done."[13] The 360 had somehow been maneuvered through the hotel's kitchen, its physical progress assisted by chefs in aprons and tall white hats as it made its way to the freight elevator. Reassembled and polished in the Waldorf's Grand Ballroom, it served as a gleaming centerpiece when Hiller board member Francis Callery hosted influential financiers, many of them his friends and former associates. Because of the postwar aviation boom-gone-bust, however, neither this convivial persuasion nor the transcontinental flight itself succeeded in enlisting the support of the East Coast financial community.

California, a huge agricultural producer, soon boasted more Hiller helicopters than did any other state. Regional promotion was simpler than were long-range efforts, but the introduction of any new product forces its manufacturer to persuade potential customers that they suddenly need something without which they have been perfectly happy. The greatest challenge to a company is accurately identifying its potential customers; once that has been done, as it was in California, the rest falls into place.

United Helicopters addressed this requirement with energy and imagination. First, they demonstrated that helicopters often make better crop dusters than do airplanes; fertilizers and insecticides sprayed by airplanes merely settle onto the tops of plants, whereas the 360's rotor downwash of almost two million

cubic feet of air per minute produced even mixing for a uniform coating above and below the leaf. Second, Hiller went the extra mile by conceiving and demonstrating new uses for agricultural helicopters such as "fig shaking" (harvesting fig trees with rotor downwash) or hastening the drying of raisins and other sun-dried fruits.

As it had in fund raising, promotion now played a major role in marketing. Things did not always proceed according to plan, however. One cold winter day, Hiller, Washburn, and marketing man Ed Rice boarded a preproduction 360 for a scheduled promotional helicopter flight to their first distributor in California, a customer in Sacramento. Lowering clouds and ground fog soon trapped the helicopter between gray layers, and a heavy rain began. Rotor downwash and the craft's forward tilt blew prodigious volumes of water into the open cockpit, pooling it behind the windscreen. Being lost, trapped over fog, and on the verge of having to start bailing added considerably to the day's misery.

Fortunately, visibility beneath the helicopter improved sufficiently for Hiller to land in a rural backyard, where a terrified occupant truly believed she was being descended upon by visitors from Mars. Mouth agape, she pointed speechless when Hiller asked her the way to Sacramento.

During another stop on the outskirts of Sacramento, Washburn fell into a hole that had been dug for a septic tank. The hapless trio nonetheless took off again, but wild gesticulations from the people below seemed to be more than waves of farewell. They descended to hover just above the ground while Rice leaned over to inspect the underside of the craft. "You won't believe it," he reported tersely. "We've lost the nose wheel."[14] Sure enough, a missing retaining screw had allowed the wheel to slip off the axle and dangle from its centering scissor.

After hasty repairs, the team took off in the rain, arriving at last at their destination, a posh Sacramento country club. They were anything but presentable. Unkempt and soaked to the skin, they found their Sacramento distributor waiting, but nobody else. The bad weather had kept everyone away, reporters included, effectively preempting the planned ceremony. It was the last straw for Rice. He refused to fly back with Hiller and Washburn, preferring to take the train to Palo Alto.

Not long afterward, an early Hiller customer had a strange experience in another 360. While flying at night over Lafayette, California, he was shaken to hear the song "Don't Roll Them Bloodshot Eyes at Me" booming at him from the dark. Much to his relief, he later learned that teenage pranksters had broken into a local church and had piped the recording at ear-splitting volume through a sound system ordinarily used to simulate chimes in the steeple.

Hiller 360s would soon find their way to other states, as well as to Puerto Rico and Hawaii (the latter still a territory). In New York, a float-mounted Hiller 360 whisked Port Authority personnel from downtown Manhattan to outlying facilities; another flew scenic tours through the Grand Canyon; and yet another 360 surveyed cane fields for a sugar company in Hawaii.

At this juncture, Stanley Hiller's role changed again. Having built a corporate structure, won certification, and commenced production, he now had a new and even more difficult challenge: simply stated, he had to achieve profitability. How does one put a company in the black? Entrepreneurs in every industry had accomplished more or less what Hiller had so far, only to fail at the day-to-day running of their companies. Drawing from experience gained running Hiller Industries a decade earlier, and fascinated with all aspects of business, Hiller successfully made this transition.

A single fateful event boosted Hiller sales more than any calculated promotion. On Sunday, 31 July 1949, twelve-year-old Terence Hallinan was thrown from a horse and knocked unconscious in the High Sierra of Yosemite National Park. It took the park's doctor eleven hours on horseback from the nearest road to reach him at Benson Lake, a body of water 8,100 feet above sea level. His examination in the remote wilderness disclosed that "Kayo," as the boy was nicknamed, had suffered a skull fracture and could not be brought out by horse or on foot. The boy would remain unconscious for three days.

A Navy plan to employ a tandem-rotor Piasecki fell by the wayside when the military services realized that none of their helicopters could in fact effect such a rescue. The Air Force considered using an amphibious Grumman SA-16A Albatross twin-engine aircraft on the water despite Benson Lake's small size. High winds and rarefied air made getting to the craterlike lake risky enough; the greater challenge still lay in taking off again with the boy

*T*he Hiller 360 was the first helicopter
used by the fishing industry. Here
a 360 lifts off from the helipad of a
tuna clipper.

58

aboard and climbing 2,000 feet almost vertically to clear the more than 10,000-foot surrounding peaks. But a human life was at stake and every effort had to be made.

Two days after the accident, having stripped his Bell Model 47 helicopter of every possible ounce of removable weight, Fresno-based helicopter pilot Knute Flint climbed to 8,000 feet before severe mountain downdrafts forced him to abandon his attempt. A former Army major and noted flier who had demonstrated the Sikorsky R-4 in China during the war, Flint was everybody's popular hero. His test flight proved, however, that winds and altitude were too much; the little Bell simply lacked sufficient performance to take off at 8,000 feet with any added load.

Upon landing, a glum Knute Flint categorically informed the awaiting crowd that neither a helicopter nor any other type of aircraft could land at Benson Lake. His description of "high, perpendicular cliffs surrounding the lake" also prompted the Air Force to abandon its unworkable Albatross rescue plan.[15] For the moment, at least, it seemed that Kayo Hallinan's only hope for rescue had failed.

New help, though, was on the way from Palo Alto. At the urging of test pilot Jay Demming, a standard Hiller 360 (UH-12) helicopter was pulled from the production line and trucked to Yosemite. At 8:00 A.M. on the day following Flint's attempt, the Hiller team arrived at the White Wolf Ranger Station, where Chief Ranger Oscar Sedergren escorted them to the end of the mountain road. On this improvised landing field they assembled the Hiller 360 in just thirty minutes.

Members of the press had been camping out at White Wolf Lodge at the base of the twenty-two-mile trail climbing to Benson Lake. By now cynical about aerial rescue efforts, they nevertheless found their hopes bolstered by the matter-of-fact approach of this new group with the shiny little helicopter. They gathered to watch as Demming rose into the air for a test hop to study the terrain; on returning he described it as "worse than a washboard."[16]

Demming made another flight an hour later. "I climbed to 10,000 feet and flew to within about five miles of the lake to survey the area and determine the course," he told anxious reporters. "I might have tried the rescue then but it was getting warm and the air was too rough to risk setting down at the lake side."[17]

Demming, a former military test pilot, decided to try again at first light when the air was still. Slightly built, disarmingly boyish with a baseball cap and an easy grin, he hardly fit the image of the dauntless rescue pilot. Nor did his elegant helicopter look capable of succeeding where even the nation's military services had failed. Nevertheless, few people at White Wolf Lodge slept much before Demming's appointed 4:20 A.M. takeoff time.

With stars showing in a pale sky scarcely bright enough to see by, Jay Demming climbed aboard the open craft wearing a heavy jacket and gloves against rotor downwash. He climbed strongly away and the Hiller's echoing beat soon

Badly injured in Yosemite's High Sierra in July 1949, twelve-year-old Terence Hallinan is rescued by Hiller test pilot Jay Demming. Courtesy T. Hallinan.

faded in the towering hills. By radio, those gathered at the takeoff site learned that he had landed successfully on the lake's narrow beach thirty-six minutes later. With young Hallinan strapped securely beside him, Demming lifted off and jettisoned the 360's thirty-seven pound battery and all but the fuel he would need for the return flight, which he accomplished without difficulty. The trip lasted just twenty-two minutes and the entire operation had taken less than an hour. "This is nifty!" the elated youth was heard to say as he was bundled into a waiting ambulance.[18]

Demming's Yosemite rescue provided for the first time a dramatic comparison of the Hiller 360 (UH-12) with the Bell Model 47. It had a strong effect on company sales, beginning with an immediate surge of orders from previously undecided customers, many of them foreign. Because of the Palo Alto group's pioneering cultivation of export markets, international sales became so brisk that by the early 1950s UH-12s were to be found in Canada, England, France, Italy, Switzerland, Belgium, Mexico, Guatemala, Venezuela, Brazil, Indochina, Pakistan, the Philippines, Egypt, Siam, and Madagascar. Hiller's sales, in fact, accounted for more than half the world's then very meager consumption of commercial helicopters.

The point must be made that although widespread, such use represented a small market indeed, and United Helicopters was as yet losing money with every commercial helicopter it sold, as were Bell and Sikorsky. Rotary-wing flight was by no means universally accepted, as was evidenced by a letter United Helicopters received from a prominent publisher early in 1951: "Gentlemen: I am sorry I do not know a thing about helicopters. I have just been warned again not to use one between my farm and Chicago."[19] The narrow commercial market widened slightly with every sale, however, as those Hillers in service quickly demonstrated their versatility across a broad spectrum of roles.

Henry J. Timken of the Timken Roller Bearing Company of Canton, Ohio, visited both Bell and Hiller in 1949, bringing with him a metallurgist as well as his personal pilot. Himself a pilot and aviation pioneer, Timken bought a Hiller 360 on the basis of his careful on-site evaluations. So did John Crummy, founder of the Food Machinery Company (FMC); after turning FMC over to his son-in-law, the adventurous businessman flew across Africa in his Hiller 360 *Congo Wasp* in the first crossing of that continent by helicopter.

Aggressively marketing Hiller 360s throughout Europe, Helicop-Air of Paris quickly became the new helicopter's leading foreign sales agent. French Air Force officer Commandant Henri Boris, who formed the company in May 1949, had come to Palo Alto a month later to add a helicopter rating to his considerable fixed-wing experience. Boris flew with the Free French out of England during World War II, often into occupied France on covert operations. Many of Helicop-Air's officers were rumored to be Boris's fellow resistance fighters from the war.

In late May 1949, two months before the Yosemite rescue, Helicop-Air sold two Hiller 360s to the French government for use in that country's losing war

*M*ilan-based Elicottero Lavoro Aereo
delivers mail to Pisa, Italy, by Hiller.

Hiller test pilot James Meade contemplates another mode of transportation in Pakistan's Sind Desert, where 360s combatted hordes of locusts.

*S*ensationalism reaches new heights
over Paris as trapeze artist André Jan
dangles from a Helicop-Air 360.

to retain Indochina as a territorial posses-sion. Helicopter rescues during World War II had been irregular and few in number; to these two French Hiller 360s, therefore, goes the honor of flying histo-ry's first routine evacuations of wounded under combat conditions.

Two courageous individuals, Lieuten-ant A. Santini and Captain Valérie André, gained international prominence in the French Army's Helicopter Rescue Sec-tion. The former was its daring leader; the latter a combat surgeon dedicated to saving lives. Not content merely to treat those patients brought to her, Captain André (who later became the first woman general in the French Army) parachuted down to help wounded soldiers. Although this dramatic approach saved lives, it meant that the wounded had to be treated on the spot rather than in well-equipped operating rooms.When the Hiller 360 helicopters arrived, therefore, Dr. André herself used them to perform countless daring rescues—at times up to seven a day—often under enemy fire.

Lieutenant Santini (whom she later married) gave Captain André advanced training following her initial instruction in France in 1949 under J. Alan Bristow, an Englishman who would himself play a role in the Indochina conflict. Having lost his job testing license-built Sikorskys at Westland Helicopters in England (reportedly for tapping the company president on the nose), Bristow found himself free to accept a position with Hiller offered through Helicop-Air. Fol-lowing his teaching duties in France and a quick trip to Egypt to demonstrate Hil-lers there, Bristow traveled to Vietnam to oversee assembly of the two French 360s that had arrived aboard ship.

Rather than merely testing helicopters, Bristow helped to launch an effective air-evacuation service, for which he was awarded the *Croix de guerre*. To the great distress of Henri Boris, Bristow also fre-quently took it upon himself to lecture top French generals, at length and uncharitably, on their conduct of the war. In later years, the irrepressible English-man would found Bristow Helicopters in England, which would become the largest helicopter operator in the world.

Back at Palo Alto, meanwhile, an improved Hiller 360 called the Model 12A (UH-12A) received supplemental certification on 8 May 1950 and immedi-ately entered production. It featured new rotor blades and a gross weight increase from 2,247 pounds to 2,400 pounds. Altogether, 194 Hiller 360s and UH-12As would be built before production ended in favor of improved models.

Then, on 25 June 1950, North Korea invaded South Korea and America suddenly found itself at war for the second time in less than five years. Already an operator of Bell helicopters, the U.S. Army now turned also to Hiller to meet an expand-ing need for rotorcraft. For the next three years, therefore, military rather than civil requirements would shape the Palo Alto company's fortunes.

Army aviation had a humble birth attached to the Signal Corps before it split off to burgeon under a succession of names. Known as the Army Air Service

*F*rench troops north of Thai Binh, Vietnam, watch as a Hiller 360 removes casualties to a hospital in Hanoi. Begun in 1949, these French combat operations marked the first routine use of helicopters for medical evacuation.

*N*ot content merely to treat the wounded
soldiers brought to her, Dr. Valérie
André learned to pilot helicopters,
performing daring rescue missions, often
under enemy fire. Courtesy V. André.

in World War I, and as the Army Air Corps in the lean years between the wars, it became hugely powerful during World War II as the Army Air Forces. By then it was relatively autonomous and largely strategic in nature; it provided tactical fighter/bomber support to ground forces but was otherwise poorly equipped to address the immediate needs of battlefield commanders. The Army's ground forces, in short, found they needed airplanes of their own.

A 1942 intraservice agreement gave the ground forces a new class of light aircraft called *liaison planes*. These low-power machines—military versions of the Piper Cub and other civil light planes—performed reconnaissance, artillery spotting, and rescues; shuttled personnel and supplies; took generals aloft to survey the lines; and otherwise proved invaluable to the American war effort. Capable of operating from unimproved fields a few hundred feet long and adept at surviving fighter attacks by turning tightly at the last moment, these liaison planes earned fame where few military planners had believed they could even survive.

After the war, the Army Air Forces became the independent U.S. Air Force under the National Security Act of 1947. The restructuring stripped from the Army almost everyone who knew anything about aviation. Thus crippled from within, organic Army aviation received another blow the following year.

The Key West Accord of 21 April 1948, a document intended to define the missions and responsibilities of the military services, extended the 1942 agreement so that the postwar Army was limited to unarmed light aircraft with gross weights of 5,000 pounds or less. The new USAF, it seemed, did not want its turf trespassed upon by the Army; it had exerted strong pressure to retain the limits and would continue to oppose Army aviation in the future.

The gross weight restriction—which applied to rotary-wing as well as fixed-wing aircraft—clearly left the postwar Army in a difficult position. As the one service which more than any other stood to benefit from helicopters of all sizes, it found itself limited by political considerations to having little helicopters useful only as trainers and flying ambulances.

To deny the Army large helicopters was to deny it utility. Able to overfly rivers and other natural barriers, capable of landing anywhere, transport helicopters could speedily move troops and supplies to strategic areas on either side of the lines; enough of them could extend the distance mechanized Army troops covered in a day from 150 to 600 miles. An additional Key West prohibition against Army aircraft carrying offensive armament was not immediately bothersome, since helicopters as yet lacked sufficient performance to serve as gunships. The handwriting was on the wall, however; a modern army without helicopters would find itself as crippled as a cavalry without horses.

Ironically, the Army's commanders—many of whom had cavalry roots—failed to appreciate these facts. The infantry-oriented leadership had heaved a collective sigh of relief with the formation of the USAF, for in the eyes of the ground-pounders the fly boys had come to exercise far too much control upon Army policy. After their departure, an emotional "good riddance" attitude toward aviation prevailed among the remaining top brass which further sabotaged, this time from within, any prospects for "organic" air power.

Just the opposite was true in the service's middle ranks, where helicopters were wanted regardless of political considerations. Chafing at arbitrary constraints, impatient with official short-sightedness, the Army's field commanders and tactical-level officers worked from· within to promote Army aviation. In this effort they were assisted by the fledgling helicopter industry, which logically viewed the Army as a potentially huge customer.

Sikorsky, Bell, Piasecki, and Hiller in fact took it upon themselves to participate in "educational" forums, arranged by far-seeing officers like helicopter proponent Colonel William F. Bunker, and otherwise foster helicopter awareness. Hiller at times provided helicopters to the Army—at company expense and with the Hiller logo painted out—on special occasions when their utility might best be demonstrated.

The outbreak of the Korean War in the summer of 1950 began right away to erode Key West constraints upon Army flight. One immediate consequence was a huge increase in the Army's appropriation for aircraft procurement, which for fiscal year 1951 jumped twentyfold from $2 million to $42,376,230. Having funds did not mean that helicopters were immediately available, however, since new production orders could not be filled

overnight. Worse still, with gross weight limits still firmly in place, all that the Army could buy in the way of rotorcraft was more little helicopters.

The U.S. Air Force, Navy, and Marines, and even British forces, had troop and transport helicopters in Korea but the U.S. Army did not. Eventually, combat losses and operational reversals directly attributable to their lack brought this disastrous situation to the attention of U.S. policy makers, who removed the 5,000-pound gross weight restriction. Although large Army helicopters did reach Korea, they arrived too late to play a meaningful role (see pages 84–87).

In late September 1950, Army Field Forces Major John Oswalt accepted delivery at Palo Alto of the Army's first Hiller YH-23 (serial no. 50-1254). Essentially a stock Model 12A equipped with military radios and enclosed litter carriers, this "air ambulance" was shipped by air to Fort Bragg, North Carolina, for accelerated evaluation owing to wartime urgency. Its success prompted production orders totaling 105 H-23As at the end of 1950.

Because the Army had lost a mechanism for direct aircraft procurement in the 1947 split, it now placed these orders through the Navy. The latter service had itself evaluated a Hiller 12A (BuNo. 125532) at NAS Patuxent River and, favorably impressed, had placed an order for sixteen trainer versions designated HTE-1. Because of the war effort, the Navy deferred to the Army, and many HTE-1s were converted right on the

Major John Oswalt (center) *accepts delivery of Hiller YH-23, ser. no. 50-1254, from Stanley Hiller, Jr., in September 1950. Lieutenant Wayne W. Eggert* (left) *of the Flight Test Division at Wright-Patterson Air Force Base, Ohio, was acceptance test pilot.*

*T*he success of the YH-23 in accelerated
Army tests led to an order for 105 Hiller
H-23As, some of which are shown here.

assembly line into H-23As. This was not so simple as it sounds. The Air Force and the Army shared a common serial numbering system, whereas the Navy used its separate "bureau" numbers. Therefore, these Navy-procured Army helicopters were accepted by, and technically briefly belonged to, the U.S. Air Force.

Direct procurement would eventually replace this cumbersome roundabout process in the early 1960s. Not so easily cured would be the U.S. Army's chronic misunderstanding of aviation missions and priorities dating back to the split with the Air Force in 1947. This internal confusion remains a significant problem to this day, as is evidenced by the Army's jumbled procurement record.

Except for floor-mounted control sticks, the Navy's HTE-1 and the Army's H-23A were basically stock Hiller 12As in military paint, powered by the same 178-hp engine as their civil counterparts. In stateside training use, these machines would prove economical and reliable once their initial technical troubles were resolved.

The same could not be said of the H-23As shipped directly to Korea in the opening days of 1951. Too lightly constructed for front-line use under adverse combat conditions, and lacking sufficient power to do all that was expected of them after having been overloaded with heavy radios and other military equipment, these first-generation 360s were found wanting in both performance and dependability. A lack of adequate field support compounded the problem, for technical and service representatives (the term for factory support personnel)

and spare parts were in decidedly short supply.

Hiller test pilot Philip T. Johnston—who would later test the Hiller Flying Platform (see chapter 5)—went to Korea with the first H-23As to give Army evacuation pilots additional flight training. His terse summary of the experience upon his return to Palo Alto said it all: "I was there; it was cold; damned glad to be back!"[20]

"We were naive," Hiller later observed of his company's failure to provide adequate field support. "We didn't understand at first why we had only one tech rep in Korea and Bell had a slew of them. They knew that to maintain those ships they would have to have good tech reps with lots of spare parts. The Army didn't know it, but Bell knew it and was able to talk them into it; we didn't know it and therefore couldn't talk them into it."[21]

Although H-23As saved hundreds of lives, their availability rate was significantly lower than that of the workhorse Bell H-13B. In performance, both aircraft—and all helicopters of that era—left something to be desired; none could be expected to maintain altitude on hot, high-density-altitude days when overloaded with pilot, two wounded, and military equipment. In retrospect, had the Hiller team had another year of production experience before war broke out, the majority of these technical problems might well have been avoided. In the urgency of war, however, the company directed its energies toward immediate improvement in two areas.

First, the availability of spare parts and other logistical support was upgraded,

This plant view shows Army H-23As in final assembly. These first-generation Hillers proved too lightly built and low-powered to be completely satisfactory under combat conditions.

*T*he Golden Gate Bridge provides a
dramatic background to H-23Bs of the
30th Engineer Aviation Detachment
based at Crissy Field in San Francisco's
Presidio. Courtesy NASM/SI.

and additional factory representatives were trained and sent to Korea. It was rough duty for men like Hiller's Edward A. Nicponsky, a civilian who spent six months living under the same difficult conditions as the helicopter detachments he helped. All but forgotten today, these tech reps from Bell and Hiller indirectly saved thousands of lives.

Second, Hiller assigned top priority to developing a second-generation helicopter, incorporating the hard-won lessons of battle. To facilitate this process, the company sought and received interservice agreement on changes to be specified for the new helicopter during a three-day Army/Navy/USAF engineering conference hosted in Palo Alto in April 1951.

A fifth American helicopter company joined Sikorsky, Bell, Piasecki, and Hiller in meeting the wartime needs for military helicopters. Kaman Helicopters in Connecticut was now building intermediate-size machines with intermeshing rotors as developed by Flettner in Germany during World War II. As the war geared up, the need for a six-to-eight passenger helicopter with internal litter-carrying ability became clear to all five companies.

Hiller responded in 1951 by proposing the Model 720, which combined—as its name implied—the dynamic components of two 360s in a new body. This unusual approach was rejected because the Army doubted the company's ability to sustain a new line of production and still meet existing orders, and also because the proposal came at a time when H-23As in Korea were plagued with maintenance problems.

At the start of 1951 the factory at Palo Alto had converted entirely to military production with commercial orders deferred because of the national emergency. New hirings (needed to support a production rate of one helicopter per day, the maximum then possible) now necessitated the acquisition of a second facility two miles north in nearby Redwood City, to which many company functions and personnel were transferred.

By now, the company was used to being called "Hiller Helicopters" by the public at large (either "Hiller Aircraft" or "United Helicopters" was correct, but not the appealingly alliterative alternative). By 1950, therefore, the huge lettering "United Helicopters, Inc." on the Palo Alto factory had given way to "Hiller Helicopters," a change unanimously endorsed at the Fifth Annual Stockholders Meeting of 9 March 1951. This meeting showed just how far the company had come: a rented circus tent was now required to accommodate some 5,800 stockholders.

Hiller's objective in founding his company, simply stated, was profitability. With the precarious hand-to-mouth early phase of its existence now past, he could look back with pride upon having given his stockholders real return on investment. Those who would stay with him in the coming years, moreover, would have no reason to regret it. There would be losing years, but the overall trend would remain one of constant increase in value (with two jumps to new plateaus as Hiller's company became associated with Electric Autolite and Fairchild, as detailed later in this book).

At this same 1951 stockholders meeting, Hiller received approval for a major expansion of the Palo Alto facility to be

Reserve pilots from NAS Oakland practice landings in an HTE-2 aboard the USS Philippine Sea *late in 1952.*

financed by a $2.5 million debenture issue arranged through Charles Blyth & Company. Construction began with a ceremonial ground breaking near the existing factory on 13 June 1951.

Almost immediately, the construction crew discovered an ancient Indian burial ground. Work halted while archaeologists summoned from nearby Stanford University had a field day unearthing artifacts and skeletons buried in the sitting position. The skeletons were intact except for crushed skulls, caused in more recent times by harrows and other farm equipment.

In July a greatly improved second-generation military helicopter prototype was lashed to the ground at Palo Alto and was run for one hundred hours at full power. It passed this test with flying colors, as it did a series of drops to test the two new landing gears replacing the 360's original "tricycle" gear, four wheels for the Navy HTE-2 and maintenance-free skids for the Army H-23B. While others had toyed with the idea of using skids instead of wheels, credit for first doing so goes to Arthur Young who—although he was no longer associated with Bell—had suggested that the company introduce them on the Model 47D as a weight-saving measure.

With a more powerful Franklin engine uprated to an even 200 hp, the new Hiller offered improved performance despite the hundred-pound increase in gross weight necessitated by its beefier structure (see Appendix A for specifications). By September 1951 the H-23B was in flight test; two months later the first production "B" models were accepted by the Army.

Two pieces of stateside news, meanwhile, offset to a degree the daunting reports of Hiller helicopter troubles in Korea. First, the Army announced in September that H-23As operating in the United States had achieved a remarkable 95 percent reliability rate. In contrast to the Korean machines, however, these stateside Hillers enjoyed ample spares and were operated within their design gross weight limits. The second bit of good news concerned Operation Southern Pine, a three-week military exercise held in October 1951 at Fort Bragg, North Carolina, in which Hiller H-23As participated. This operation brilliantly validated the concept of helicopter support of military ground forces. Coupled with the real-life lessons learned in Korea, Southern Pine worked a profound change upon the Army, which henceforth adopted helicopters in a variety of tactical roles.

Then there was the splendid record of the 30th Engineer Base Topographic Battalion, which from 1950 through 1955 conducted yearly summer expeditions to Alaska to map that territory (Alaska would become a state in 1959). Based at Crissy Field at San Francisco's Presidio in the shadow of the Golden Gate Bridge, the 30th Topographic Battalion's aviation detachment initially operated Bell H-13s, which they traded after one year for Hiller H-23As. Crissy Field base commander Major James R. Hodge headed the 30th, assisted by Captain Leo Bellieu (operations officer), Captain John Martin (administrative officer), and Lieutenant Harry Jones (engineering officer/test pilot). Beginning in 1951, when the unit adopted Hillers, technical representative Nicholas Hart accompanied the 30th to

Alaska to troubleshoot during maintenance in the field.

Using these aircraft and the newer B models, which began arriving in 1952, the 30th covered vast stretches of virgin wilderness. By 1954, the 30th Engineer Group (as it was redesignated) had standardized on Hiller H-23Bs because of their ruggedness and safety. From April through September of that year, the group logged some 8,000 accident-free flight hours with forty-four H-23Bs.

"I flew Bells and Hillers under totally adverse weather conditions, and I preferred the Hiller by far," recalls Leo Bellieu, who took command of the 30th during the course of its Alaskan activities. "Having flown it in 55- to 65-mph winds, I came to trust and love it dearly."[22]

Shortly before the 1951 expedition, 30th Battalion pilot George Brockway established an interesting if unofficial record in a civil 360 fitted with H-23A-style floor-mounted control sticks. Accompanied by Hiller test pilot Jim Meade, Captain Brockway took off from San Francisco on a routine training flight and trimmed for a 60-mph cruise. On impulse, he decided to see how long the Hiller would fly along by itself. To their amazement, neither man had to touch the cyclic, collective, rudder pedals, or throttle for over two hours.

On the engineering front, Hiller undertook pioneering rotor-tip damper research under Air Force contract AF 33(600)-29488 at the start of the 1950s. Housed in the blades to control an articulated tip was a harmonic aerodynamic damper, devised by Hiller engineers to flatten out the undulating track of deflection-prone helicopter rotor blades. Reducing blade-bending stresses would produce a smoother ride. The advanced concept of tracking the rotor blade tips onto an even plane was far ahead of its time; NASA and the helicopter industry would return to it almost forty years later.

A costly mistake shook Hiller Helicopters early in 1952, shortly before the Hiller H-23B entered service. As it expanded, the company's ranks had been augmented by senior staff arriving from declining segments of the fixed-wing industry. Several executives newly arrived from Convair (the interim name of Consolidated-Vultee Aircraft, today General Dynamics) took it upon themselves to try to dictate terms and conditions to the U.S. Navy—with disastrous results.

There were perhaps occasions during World War II when giant companies like the San Diego–based Convair—builder of the B-24 Liberator heavy bomber—could get away with such high-handed and dictatorial behavior. For a small fledgling company to presume to tell Uncle Sam where to get off, though, was a far different matter. Even with the Korean War in full swing in the early 1950s, excess aircraft production capacity remained from World War II. In short, the Navy could—and did—go elsewhere for its light helicopters after buying thirty-five HTE-2s. Twenty more of this model were built with U.S. Mutual Defense Assistance Program (MDAP) funds early in 1953 for use by the British Royal Navy, which designated the type HT.1.

This costly error, for which Stanley Hiller assumed ultimate responsibility,

Oregon operator Dean Johnson, an early user of Hillers, readies a 12-B for once-a-year duty as Santa's sleigh. A hopper-equipped Hiller and some Piper Super Cubs in the background hint at normal duties of a more rugged nature.

Hiller test pilot and marketing executive Robert Boughton plots an aerial reelection campaign tour with U.S. Senator Deneen Watson of Illinois. Philip D. Armour IV (right) of Chicago-based Armour Meat Company provides the helicopter.

precipitated a major board-level confrontation and forced the resignation of most of the Convair contingent. For Hiller, the event was a keen disappointment; because of his own misplaced faith in the Convair executives, his company now needed restructuring and new people had to be brought in. At a very busy juncture, Hiller was forced not only to reassume duties he had earlier relinquished but also to spend much time talking to Navy leaders in and around Washington, D.C. In his late twenties, Hiller had hit what he recalls as his personal low-point in the running of his own aircraft company.

The loss of its second-largest military customer had, in fact, diminished the prospects of Hiller Helicopters. Despite its president's efforts at fence-mending, real damage had been done, and it would be ten more years before the company received mainstream Navy support for a production contract. In between, the only Navy contracts received would be issued by the Office of Naval Research and the Bureau of Aeronautics' power plant division. However interesting, these research-oriented programs—described later in this book—would not generate volume production.

In March 1952, lessening military demands permitted the resumption of some commercial production with deliveries to begin in June. The bulk of backlogged civil orders, however, would not be addressed until after hostilities ceased in July 1953. Customers who had patiently waited for up to three years for their Hillers were now rewarded with the greatly improved UH-12B, a civil version of the Army H-23B. The new commercial helicopter—offering a fully enclosed cabin, electric trim, and a skid landing gear—sold for $36,400. Good as it was, the best was yet to come in this series of commercial helicopters.

Newer Hillers, meanwhile, were now evacuating wounded in Indochina. Having received four H-23As early in 1952, the French Army's rescue squadron now received three H-23Bs at the beginning of March 1953. With enough power to really perform in Vietnam's hot climate, the "B" model—proclaimed a "veritable little miracle" by Dr. Valérie André—was a substantial improvement over the earlier machines.[23] In the year remaining before the French-Vietnamese truce, it proved reliable, in sharp contrast to the squadron's troublesome new Westland-built Sikorsky S-51s.

Of 273 "B" models procured in 1951, roughly half were shipped to Korea. The remainder remained stateside to join the Army's new Primary Helicopter School. In all, 453 H-23B/HTE-2/UH-12B series helicopters would be produced between 1952 and 1955. The 500th Hiller production helicopter—a milestone celebrated in September 1953—was, appropriately enough, a U.S. Army H-23B, for the Army was still Hiller's biggest customer. By now, military Hillers also flew with the British Royal Navy, French Air Force, and Swiss Army. Holland, Canada, and Thailand's air and police forces would also soon be flying H-23s.

Carrying dogs to locate buried survivors, Swiss H-23Bs rescued avalanche victims in the Alps following heavy snowstorms in January 1954. In the same part of the world some months later, a U.S. Army helicopter pilot plucked a familiar-looking flood victim off a roof-

top in Bavaria. "Didn't I bring you out a few hours ago?" he asked the German. "Yes," the latter replied in accented English, "I enjoy riding a helicopter and so I went back by row boat."[24] The number of helicopter rescues worldwide had, in fact, risen to the point where they no longer necessarily generated newspaper headlines. The novelty, it seemed, was wearing thin.

How had Korea affected Hiller Helicopters? The impact of the conflict on the company is perhaps best illustrated by the increase in annual gross sales: The total for 1949—the first full year of sales—was $557,000. That figure rose to $1,262,000 in 1950 when war broke out, then jumped fivefold to $6,657,000 the following year. In 1952, it reached $14,399,000—fully twenty-five times the volume of just four years earlier.

After the high-level wartime production, total sales dipped to a little over $6 million in 1954 before climbing steadily upward again to over $16 million by 1959. In 1950s dollars, this level of sales meant that Hiller had outgrown the "small business" label which had so hindered its military procurement efforts. Pentagon perceptions proved difficult to change, however, and Hiller Helicopters was still vastly smaller than fixed-wing giants such as Boeing, Convair, Douglas, Lockheed, or McDonnell.

In September 1953 the Hiller company

Tokyo's Ginza provides a backdrop to Japan's first commercial helicopter, a 12-B purchased in 1952 by the Sangyo Keizai Shimbun publishing company.

acquired production rights to the Doman LZ-5, a six-to-eight passenger helicopter combining German Flettner patents with inventor Glidden Doman's own advanced semirigid four-blade rotor. The Army had shown an interest in Doman's work. A proposed Army version of the craft, the Doman YH-31, had already flown on 17 April 1953.

The Doman acquisition was engineered by then-Colonel William F. Bunker of the Army's Transportation Corps. With H-23 production declining after the Korean War, Bunker felt such an arrangement desirable to maintain the health of Hiller Helicopters and, by extension, the Army's production base.

Hiller was pleased with the prospect of producing the Doman LZ-5 because he realized that his company would always be at a disadvantage competing head-to-head against Bell, which enjoyed greater funding and acceptance. It made sense to develop new products not directly competitive with Bell. Between the three-seat Bells and Hillers, and the much bigger Sikorskys and Piaseckis, there was still a gap in the helicopter market only partially addressed by Kaman. Doman's promising design was the right size to fill it.

In the end, however, a shift in post-Korea Army priorities put an end to the project. The Doman YH-31 was shelved before it could enter production in Palo Alto. An improved Doman-Fleet LZ-5-2 subsequently flew in Canada. Briefly considered by the Army, it was dropped in 1957 because the newer Bell XH-40 (later redesignated UH-1 Iroquois) showed greater promise.

During the war in Vietnam, helicopters

would play a major role. But the Hiller company ceased to exist in the early days of the Vietnamese conflict and produced no helicopters for it, although some H-23s did see service there. The Hiller story is inextricably entwined with Korea, not with America's war in Vietnam. The following brief overview of the Army's use of helicopters in Korea is of particular interest in this regard.

The U.S. Army began operations in Korea in the summer of 1950 with fixed-wing aircraft such as the Stinson L-5 and the North American L-17. The former was a World War II liaison plane and the latter, a general aviation four-seater minimally suited to military use. It was immediately obvious that helicopters were in far too short supply.

The first helicopter evacuation of wounded was reportedly performed by a USAF H-5 in July 1950, shortly after hostilities began. Improvised evacuations by Marine Corps HO3S-1 helicopters belonging to observation squadron VMO-6 took place on 4 August 1950, during a battle near Chindongni, Korea. The Air Force, Navy, and Marines, moreover, soon had a larger and more versatile helicopter at their disposal, the Sikorsky S-55, variously designated the H-19/HO4S/HRS. Arriving in June 1951, S-55s performed transport and rescue duties, although their large size made them uneconomical for the routine evacuation of combat casualties.

Before 1950 ended, the Army had performed its first air evacuation with a Bell H-13B. In the opening weeks of 1951,

litter-equipped Bell H-13s and (in smaller numbers) Hiller H-23As were routinely removing wounded from combat zones to Mobile Army Surgical Hospital (MASH) units for lifesaving medical treatment. Each MASH unit had a helicopter detachment assigned to it consisting of four helicopters, four pilots, and four mechanics. Indicative of the hazards of this new form of combat flying, the Army's 2nd Helicopter Detachment pilots all were awarded Distinguished Flying Crosses within their first two weeks of operational flying.

Although the Army was the service with the greatest need for transport helicopters, it was denied Sikorsky H-19s of its own until the Korean War was all but over. Because of Key West restrictions, this service had to make do with light helicopters that lacked the strategic value and logistical support capability afforded by larger types. For this reason, U.S. Army operations in 1950s Korea more closely resembled those of World War II than those of 1960s–1970s Vietnam.

To offset the crippling lack of large helicopters, additional airplanes capable of short and rough field operations were pressed into service. In the spring of 1951 came the Cessna L-19 Bird Dog, a two-plane tandem version of that company's rugged civil Model 180. Toward the end of 1952 came the de Havilland L-20 Beaver, a capacious Canadian-built "bush" airplane capable of carrying heavy loads. But these fixed-wing types simply could not counter the Army's lack of troop and transport helicopters in Korea's rugged terrain.

This point was driven home in 1952, when a lone Bell H-13 spent five days

*A*n H-23A of the Fourth U.S. Army Helicopter Detachment lands at a Korean
MASH unit with wounded aboard. To save weight and boost marginal performance,
the Hiller's chin landing lights, direction-finding radio, and loop antenna have
been removed.

shuttling twenty-nine people and 20,300 pounds of supplies and equipment to the top of Korean Hill 1304. The materials were needed by the 65th Engineers, who were helping the 25th Infantry dig in to hold this strategic position from advancing enemy forces. Observing this historic first Army helicopter airlift, one field officer noted in disgust that it was crazy "to send a sedan to do the job of a truck."[25]

Only by late 1951 had Key West restrictions finally eased sufficiently for the Army to get helicopters weighing over 5,000 pounds. The first of an initial order for ninety-seven H-19s was delivered before the end of the year and began an accelerated service test program. The USAF now also began procuring Piasecki H-21s and H-25s for Army use (the latter a version of the Navy's HUP-1), but unlike the Sikorsky, these tandem-rotor transports—both of which saw service elsewhere in Korea—would not become operational with the Army before hostilities ended in mid-1953.

In contrast, Sikorsky H-19s of the Army's pioneering 6th Transport Helicopter Company (THC) arrived in Korea in January 1953 and flew their first combat mission in April. H-19s of both the 6th and 13th THCs participated in Operation Little Switch, a repatriation of sick and wounded UN troops starting before the war ended. Fourteen of these transport helicopters also took part in Operation Sky Hook in support of the 25th Infantry Division, carrying over a half-million pounds of supplies in just three days.

Although the accomplishments of these aircraft reinforced the value of large helicopters to Army tactical operations, their late arrival denied them a significant participation in the conflict. Consequently, the evacuation of wounded soldiers by Bell and Hiller light helicopters remains the U.S. Army's single meaningful use of rotary-wing aviation in Korea.

More than any other factor, helicopters reduced the death rate from battlefield injuries in Korea to the lowest point in the history of warfare, a rate less than half that suffered by wounded American troops in World War II. In some cases, pilots even administered plasma in flight by squeezing a pressure bulb connected to a bottle suspended in the cabin. This practice—one of many shock-trauma innovations to emerge during the war—was developed by the 2nd Helicopter Detachment itself.

By the time peace was declared on 27 July 1953, the Army had approximately 1,000 helicopters, the vast majority of which were training and evacuation types. Bell and Hiller machines (the former also used in this role by the Marines) evacuated over 20,000 American, South Korean, British, French, Ethiopian, Benelux, Thai, and Turkish troops during this conflict.

Army Lieutenant Joseph Bowler personally flew some 824 seriously wounded soldiers to field hospitals in 482 missions. And Lieutenant William P. Brake flew 900 evacuations during 545 missions. Brake, a flight engineer on Navy PBYs during World War II, had switched services in order to fly in Korea. "There's a lot of satisfaction in bringing wounded men back," he stated in 1953. "Most evacuation trips took about thirty minutes from the time the men were hit until they were in the hospital. The same trip by ambulance would sometimes take four hours, which could mean the difference between life and death."[26]

Among the toughest of Brake's many missions were six night flights, placing extraordinary demands upon his knowledge of the rugged Korean countryside and culminating in landings made by jeep headlights or flashlight. His closest call came when incorrect map coordinates took him two miles behind enemy lines; there he evaded withering small-arms fire by ducking behind a river bank and skimming away at zero altitude. The dangers Brake faced were not unique: U.S. and foreign pilots alike participating in this multinational police action pushed the newly perfected helicopter to its limits.

On the home front, meanwhile, Army Field Forces established their first helicopter transport companies in 1951 and used them in full-scale training operations at Fort Bragg, North Carolina, the following year. Troops, equipment, and supplies were all carried by the new H-19s. These exercises marked the first time that the U.S. Army ever enjoyed full helicopter tactical support.

The Army in 1952 used the Korean War's inevitable loosening of Key West constraints to adopt a twelve-battalion helicopter program calling for three battalions each of heavy and medium cargo helicopters (five- and three-ton capacity, respectively) and six battalions of light cargo machines (one and a half–ton capacity). Although Key West still imposed some weight limits, restricted operating radii, and prohibited the arming of Army helicopters, implementation of this program was a step toward development of the air mobility tactics the Army would later employ in Vietnam.

Tip-powered Helicopters

In its quarter-century existence, the Hiller helicopter company focused most of its energies in three key areas. One was the achievement of helicopter production followed by ongoing product support and improvement. Another was the successful VTOL (vertical-takeoff-and-landing) program described in chapter 5.

The third, pursued concurrently with the others, was a radically different approach to helicopter flight called "tip propulsion." As the name implies, this Hiller research-and-development program sought to power a helicopter from the tips of its rotor blades. Pursued by Hiller in various forms, this longstanding company effort was frustrated in its ultimate aim of enlisting military sponsorship for construction of giant tip-powered flying crane helicopters. The program did, however, foster the development of ingenious new power plants (including the first American-designed-and-built jet engine to be granted production certification) and aircraft (including the only tip-powered helicopters ever produced in the United States).

The idea of spinning a rotor from its tips first intrigued Stanley Hiller in 1945, but the need to get a helicopter into production—essential to his young company's survival—delayed the start of dedicated research in this area until 1947. At that juncture, with construction of the 360X just beginning, he was at last free to turn his attention to the subject of tip propulsion.

The idea, literally, was to give helicopters a "new twist" by supplying power directly where needed—to the blade tips that generate most of the lift. Hiller power plant engineers in Palo Alto were convinced this was the logical way to power a rotor, on the assumption that developing an engine to endure the rigors of tip rotation was easier than eliminating the severe weight penalties associated with conventional designs of the time.

A conventional helicopter produces power in its fuselage, passes it through a heavy transmission that steps high engine RPMs down to main rotor speeds, then sends it through shafting to the rotor head, which turns the blades by their roots. Hiller sought a simpler alternative to this roundabout approach.

In single-rotor helicopters, moreover, a significant percentage of engine power never reaches the main rotor to develop lift. Instead, it must be diverted to a tail rotor to counteract torque, which is the tendency of a helicopter to twist in opposition to the spin it imparts to its main

Hiller's rotor tip propulsion program began in 1947 with the whirling of pulse jet engines, singly and in clusters. To eliminate flapping intake valves or reeds affected by high-G whirling, derivatives achieving pulsed combustion through harmonically tuned tailpipes were developed. One of these valveless "sonic engines" appears at bottom right beside the largest pulse jet.

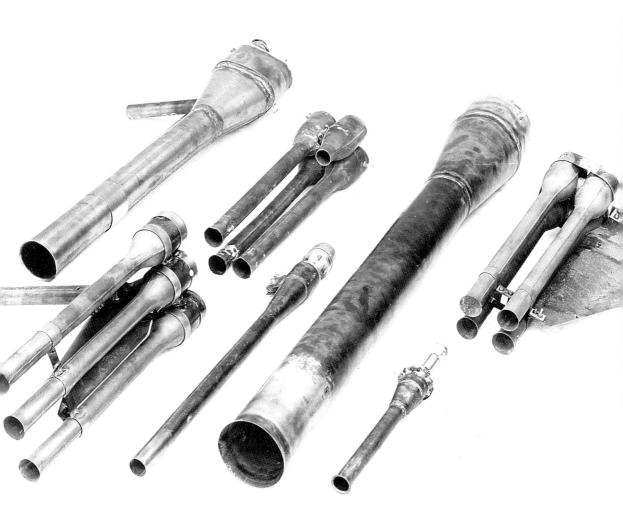

rotor. The elements needed to make a helicopter fly, in short, added weight and subtracted power to the point where critics of early production helicopters wondered—with some justification—if so little performance really warranted so much effort.

The intriguing alternative of tip propulsion offered significant advantages: First, tip-powered helicopters have no torque because the rotor spins itself instead of being acted upon from below (main-shaft bearing friction does tend to yaw the helicopter in the direction of rotation of its rotor, but this almost negligible force is easily countered). Second, the heavy transmission and vibration-prone drive shafts of conventional helicopters are eliminated. Third, engine cooling problems cease to exist. Fourth, tip engines provide more than enough tip mass for autorotational inertia and to prevent "coning" (the tendency of blades to bend upward while lifting), thus eliminating the need for the unproductive ballast carried by conventional helicopters in their blade tips (as tip jets on large-diameter rotors threatened to make them droop at rest, however, this last advantage was a mixed blessing).

Design studies by large helicopter manufacturers revealed in the 1950s that problems afflicting conventional designs grew disproportionately with size. Calculations then revealed, for example, that the transmission alone of a 33,000 pound machine—the approximate weight of an intercity passenger helicopter—would consume fully 31 percent of the aircraft's payload. Some 300 of the engine's total horsepower, in other words, would be required solely to lift that one compo-

nent. This progressive deterioration in performance dimmed prospects for very large rotorcraft.

If helicopters were to increase in size over time on a par with fixed-wing aircraft, a way to circumvent these negative scale effects was needed. Tip propulsion offered a solution because tip-powered craft actually fare *better* on a large scale since tip G loads decrease as rotor diameter increases. Giant flying crane helicopters—the ultimate exploitation of the concept—would in fact subject their engines to many times less centrifugal stress than did small tip-powered machines.

Pioneering the flying crane held promise from a business as well as a technological standpoint. "It was the right way to go for large helicopters," Hiller firmly believed. "It made economic sense to get away from the little machines; that was the driving force behind the tip-power effort."[1]

As an ongoing challenge, Hiller was exploring which engines to use to achieve tip-powered flight. Turbine power was Hiller's goal from the start, but an initial lack of jet engines small enough to power research prototypes delayed their employment by the company. In the interim, Hiller would test a wide variety of power plants ranging from pulse jets and ramjets to sophisticated derivatives developed in-house. Finally, before its program ended in the 1960s, Hiller would successfully whirl a small newly developed turbojet engine on its test rotor.

Tip power was not a new concept, of course; various European and American companies had or would embrace it. The first tip-powered helicopter to fly with any success was the Doblhoff Wn 342, built in Germany during World War II by Austrian engineer Friedrich Doblhoff. French and Dutch manufacturers would continue to experiment with various forms of tip propulsion in the postwar era. In the latter 1950s, SNCASO in France would actually produce 177 two-seat Model 1221 Djinn jet helicopters with rotors spun by compressed air.

In the postwar United States, Kellett, McDonnell, Hughes, American Helicopter, and Marquardt would all compete with Hiller in this arena. Most of these efforts would follow the European approach of ducting compressed air or hot exhaust gases through hollow blades, and thence out through cornering nozzles to spin a rotor. Although Hiller would spearhead America's evaluation of the most promising form of this European concept, the primary focus of the company's program would be another approach to tip power: mounting jet engines on the ends of a helicopter's rotor blades.

Although not the first company to pursue "tip-engine" helicopter development, Hiller would be its greatest champion for some two decades. The great majority of research contracts stemming from military interest in this intriguing concept would in fact go to Hiller. One notable result of the company's singular commitment to this concept would be the Navy HOE-1/Army YH-32 Hornet of the mid-1950s, America's only tip-powered production helicopters.

Having systematically solved or disproved real and imagined obstacles to the construction of flying cranes of phenomenal size and simplicity, Hiller in the early 1960s would win a hard-fought industry competition to build a flying crane for the U.S. Army. Teamed with jet engine maker Continental, it would be poised for success in 1965 when the Army—despite a logical requirement for such vehicles—would cancel the program before a prototype could be built.

The promising effort thus ended was only one of many heavy-lift tip-powered helicopters conceived and pursued by the company. A detailed chronology of Hiller Aircraft's tip-propulsion activities follows.

In the fall of 1944, Germany began sending hundreds of Fieseler Fi 103 pilotless aircraft over England. Better known as the V-1 (V for *Vergeltungswaffe* or "revenge weapon"), these flying bombs were nicknamed "doodlebug" by the British and "buzz bomb" by the Americans. A long tube above the buzz bomb's aft fuselage housed its pulse jet, a type of engine invented in Germany in the late 1920s. V-1s produced a window-rattling chugging in flight, accompanied by fiery flashes when viewed at night.

Once heard, the dread-inspiring noise of the V-1 could never be forgotten. Far more frightening still was the sudden silence when a preset mechanism aboard the gyroscopically guided bomb sent 2,210 pounds of high explosive plunging into whatever lay below.

Early in 1948, the few neighbors along Willow Road in Palo Alto also became acquainted with the brain-rattling clatter of pulse jets, albeit smaller ones than the German prototype. The source was the new United Helicopters facility, where the Hiller 360 commercial helicopter was being readied for production. While the press focused on the 360, a select group of company personnel "quietly" resumed tip-propulsion research, begun the year before, on a twenty-foot-diameter whirl teststand erected as far across company grounds as possible from the factory.

The teststand itself started life as a small, single-seat research prototype powered by two six-pound-thrust reed-type pulse jets. Called the Hiller TPJ-1, it was not flown. It was tested on the ground, where it provided valuable insight into aerodynamic and structural problems associated with the hostile high-G tip environment. After its conversion into a stationary whirl platform, the forgotten TPJ-1 played a critical role in the company's tip-propulsion effort.

The trio of six-pound static-thrust pulse jets spinning this outdoor rotor were scaled-down V-1 units, available from any hobby shop in 1948 for model airplane use. Although better at developing decibels than thrust, they nevertheless generated empirical data. The first problem was keeping them together and working, because high G loads tended to interfere with the operation of their shutter-valving. Slowing the rotor down alleviated this problem only at the expense of efficiency.

These unbelievably loud little units had other problems, not the least of which was their excessive length, which poorly suited them to rotor use. The project engineers therefore decided to reduce noise and length simultaneously by designing their own truncated pulse jets with multiple tuned tail pipes bristling from a single combustion chamber. A new design with five tail pipes did prove more compatible with its sensitive blade-tip location, but the clatter—although different in character—was no less loud.

Because tip-mounted engines driving a rotor by jet flow were by no means the only approach to tip propulsion, it seemed prudent to review the options before committing to this or any other line of development. Hiller's first look at tip power had been in the spring of 1945 when his company's fifteen or so employees built a tethered model with propellers at the tips of its rotor blades. An electric drill motor in the rotor head spun shafts, buried within the blades, which turned the propellers through individual gearboxes.

Some earlier experimenters had built and actually attempted to fly full-size helicopters with propeller-powered rotors. The model was sufficient to convince Hiller that this approach was unworkable for a variety of reasons, one being the gyroscopic forces produced by spinning propellers as they in turn are whirled around a rotor. It was a stress engineer's nightmare, and the Hiller team wisely steered clear of it.

At the end of World War II, U.S. military technical intelligence teams exhaustively evaluated a broad spectrum of captured enemy equipment. The U.S. Government made the results of these evaluations available to American industry in the immediate postwar era. In this manner—and directly from Hiller employees who had participated in such evaluations—the Hiller group learned of the work in Hitler's Germany of Austrian helicopter developer Friedrich Doblhoff. Doblhoff's experimental helicopters employed a compressor in the fuselage to force fuel and air through the rotor blades. The two were mixed and then ignited in rearward-angled combustion chambers at the blade tips.

Hiller's second pulse-jet effort expanded upon Doblhoff's approach to tip propulsion. The Hiller Powerblade of 1949 consisted of a pulse jet laid lengthwise within the blade root, to which air and fuel were fed through a valving assembly at the hub. The blade's hollow main spar served as an extended tail pipe and the efflux was exhausted at the tip through a cornering nozzle, which deflected the thrust aft to spin the rotor.

The helicopter industry has since termed Hiller's Powerblade—and any other pressure jet rotor with exhaust gases attaining temperatures of approximately 1,000 degrees Fahrenheit—a "hot-cycle pressure-jet" rotor. Other industry attempts to build hot-cycle helicopters would seek to spin a rotor with turbojet exhaust. And turbofan engines would mark a later development in which warm-cycle pressure-jet rotors with efflux temperatures of around 600 degrees F were tried.

Doblhoff's simpler rotor, in contrast, is today termed a cold-cycle pressure jet. To this rotor, powered by compressed air, Doblhoff added "tip burning," or external combustion at the blade tips, for added thrust. The French Djinn of the 1950s—the only helicopter ever produced with a pressure-jet rotor—used compressed air supplied by a turbine engine; it performed well enough to dispense with tip burning.

The Hiller Powerblade—the company's first government-sponsored engine development—was the world's first hot-cycle rotor. A number of Powerblades,

ranging from fourteen to twenty-eight feet in rotor diameter and producing fourteen to thirty pounds of thrust each, were fully instrumented and tested under Navy sponsorship in 1950. Their construction varied from all-steel to aluminum protected by thick thermal insulation, the challenge to Hiller engineers being to design blades that did not warp or deflect on the plane of rotation from internal heating.

Late in 1949, Hiller abandoned plans to fly a Powerblade rotor on the unflown single-seat TPJ-1 now serving as a stationary whirlstand. The reason was simple: neither Doblhoff's cold cycle nor Hiller's hot cycle approached the efficiency of an engine mounted directly at the blade tip; it was simply asking too much of a rotor to perform effectively as both wing and engine. For one thing, the approach dictated a thick blade, which is inherently less efficient aerodynamically.

The U.S. Army Air Forces had earlier contracted in 1946 with the Kellett Aircraft Corporation for development of a huge cold-cycle pressure-jet helicopter begun by Kellett as a company project during World War II. Refined at war's end with the benefit of German data, this ambitious project was sold in 1949 to the Hughes Tool Company's aviation subsidiary, builders of the gargantuan Hughes HK-1 *Spruce Goose* flying boat. The sale allowed Kellett to pay off creditors and remain in business a bit longer, but it was clear that the ailing company was living on borrowed time. To generate funds for helicopter development, Wallace Kellett had formed a commercial division with products ranging from furniture to refrigerators to new inventions of questionable value. Branching into areas far from the company's mainstream business of rotor-craft proved to be an unwise decision; rather than serving to subsidize Kellett's helicopter division, its new business interests forced the company inexorably into bankruptcy.

Designated the Hughes XH-17, the Kellett-designed aircraft made its first flight in October 1952. The stilt-legged flying crane was powered by two General Electric J35 turbojets mounted on either side of the fuselage. Topped by a rotor fully 130 feet in diameter, the XH-17 had a gross weight of 52,000 pounds and a projected payload of 27,000 pounds. Although preliminary tests showed it to be unsuccessful, interest in the unusual vehicle would remain to frustrate later Hiller efforts to build tip-turbine flying cranes for the Army. Ironically, the XH-17's parameters were originally laid out by rotary-wing aerodynamicist Wayne Wiesner before he joined Hiller.

Bob Wagner had also worked on the project before joining Hiller in 1946. Four years later, Wagner was one of several Hiller engineers hired away by Howard Hughes, who was offering exorbitant salaries. Chief of testing for the XH-17 until it failed, Wagner would work briefly as chief engineer of McCulloch Motors' Aircraft Division before returning to Hiller late in 1953.[2]

Kellett had sold the project to Hughes out of necessity, for by the close of the 1940s Kellett Aircraft was in irreversible decline. In retrospect, it is difficult to comprehend why—with years of rotary-wing experience to build on and key elements of the technology already in hand—Kellett and Pitcairn approached true helicopter development so late and so halfheartedly. Either company, had it shown leadership in this emerging field, might still be manufacturing aircraft today.

Hiller's hot-cycle Powerblade program was not wasted, for the company was now convinced that the engines themselves should be mounted right on the blade tips. Pressure-jet blades were simply too cumbersome to produce comparable efficiencies. As a result, the test program would proceed to ramjets, then to sonic engines (valveless pulse jets), and finally to true turbine power plants. In the process, Hiller would develop and test other engines not yet anticipated.

But a major obstacle to Hiller's approach to flying cranes now appeared. The National Advisory Committee for Aeronautics (NACA) put forth a baseless but persuasive argument against mounting jet engines on rotor blades. Having evaluated Hiller proposals at the request of the U.S. Navy, this government research organization asserted that pulse and ramjets—or any type of jet engine mounted on helicopter rotor blades—would suffer from "off-center burning" when centrifugal force threw the fuel-air mixture against the side of the combustion chamber farthest from the hub. This deflection, the NACA claimed, would cause engines to fail. The NACA—predecessor to NASA—further predicted that tip-mounted engines would starve each other of fresh air by whirling directly through each other's hot efflux.

Unwilling to abandon this field of study without first ascertaining whether it was indeed unworkable, Hiller undertook an exhaustive program under Navy contract which eventually proved the NACA wrong on both counts. High-speed photographs showed that off-center burning simply did not manifest itself; rather than being thrown to the side, fuel when atomized in an engine followed the airflow through the engine. Actual flight tests, meanwhile, demonstrated that tip-mounted ramjets ran into each other's exhaust only when the helicopter was on the ground or in a shallow descent, the power loss experienced in both instances being minor. Unfortunately, it took almost ten years and thousands of hours of ground and flight testing to set the record straight and to dismiss these unfounded but damaging criticisms.

McDonnell Aircraft in St. Louis and the U.S. Air Force were already partners in tip-propulsion research of their own. Their XH-20 of 1947, nicknamed *Little Henry*, was a crude test frame powered by gaseous fuel-burning ramjets at the tips of its rotor. Friedrich Doblhoff, who immigrated to the United States after World War II, was in part responsible for the XH-20, which is notable as the first use of ramjets for tip propulsion, and as the first ramjet-powered vehicle to carry a man. *Little Henry*'s engines were strictly the work of Elbert R. Sargent, a premier ramjet engineer. Tested through the early 1950s, the XH-20 was abandoned before the project goal of a successful torqueless rotor was reached. The Hiller team had followed its progress with keen interest.

The first jet-powered airplane flew in 1939, just eight years before the Palo Alto team set about mounting jets at the tips of a helicopter's rotor blades. Early tur-bojets were less than ideal for tip use. They were too thirsty, but they were bet-ter in this regard than either the pulse jets or the ramjets; low-speed ramjets in particular are truly gluttonous, guzzling some ten pounds of fuel per hour for each pound of thrust they generate.

In 1947, there were two basic types of turbojet engines to choose from: The first, the axial-flow engine, has a long, narrow shape well suited to high-speed fixed-wing flight because it presents less drag-producing frontal area. The second type is the centrifugal-flow engine. Fatter and shorter than axial-flow types, centrifugal-flow units are less prone to compressor stall. Their length also suits them better to blade-tip use.

Hiller turned to power-plant manufac-turers to see if they would be interested in adapting their centrifugal-flow turbo-jets to run while being whirled on a giant rotor. At the very least, new bearings and fuel-flow methods would be required to offset centrifugal forces. As might be expected, the Hiller inquiry generated little enthusiasm among engine builders who—faced with the NACA study and perceiving the lack of a tip-propulsion helicopter market—saw no inducement to undertake development work.

Hiller consequently proceeded with its in-house engine developments. Turbojets were out; their enormous development costs placed them beyond the means of a small company. Pulse jets had effectively been exhausted. What was left as a point of departure was the ramjet, the simplest power plant ever devised. The company's first ramjet looked like a slightly wrinkled watermelon, weighed eleven pounds, and developed thirty-one pounds of thrust. This basic athodyd (aerothermodynamic duct) had no moving parts. At high speed, air "ramming" into the front was mixed with fuel introduced through a tube, and was ignited by a stationary flame-holder to produce thrust as the expanding hot gases were expelled at the rear.

Following static tests, one of the engines was placed on a full-size whirl-stand rotor with a counterweight at the other end. The rotor was then spun fast enough for the engine to begin running on its own. Ignition was initially crude: raw gasoline was poured into the ramjet's mouth and a source of flame was tossed in. Grass and other flammable materials were often set on fire during such tests. This cumbersome system soon gave way to a special spark plug within the engine. With testing thus facilitated, the group proceeded to explore flameout and other tendencies which had given ramjets their reputation for unreliability.

In just a few years, the Hiller team headed by Harold Sigler achieved extremely high ramjet reliability. The group also made a bit of progress in reducing the ramjet's gluttonous thirst at subsonic speeds far below the hypersonic regime where ramjets are most efficient, but fuel consumption remained roughly ten times that of small reciprocating engines of comparable power (31 lbs. of thrust being equivalent to 34-hp). On the positive side, ramjets run on kerosene, alcohol, and just about anything else that burns, so cheaper fuels could be substituted for costlier high distillates like gasoline.

Construction and modification of tip-propulsion test equipment was the domain of gifted tinkerer Ed Bennett, the company's resident mechanical genius.

Bennett greatly enhanced this facility's usefulness by devising and building a free airstream source powerful enough to permit static running of ramjets. His primary source for parts was the surplus aircraft market, where he found wartime fighter-plane engines at rock-bottom prices. He purchased a number for their superchargers which, driven by up to a half-dozen commercial engines at a time, supplied a large continuous volume of air at 650 feet per second.

Building the flying ramjet-powered prototypes was far simpler than making the first Hiller 360, because of tip propulsion's inherent simplicity. Interestingly, Hiller chose to develop the jigs and tooling necessary for manufacture and then to use the first ships off the line for flight trials, rather than make "scratch-built" prototypes. When finished, the first machine was recognizable as a Hiller only by its Rotormatic paddles; in size and configuration it was unlike any other helicopter so far tested at Willow Road.

Chief test pilot Frank Peterson took the first Hiller HJ-1 Hornet, as the craft was designated, off the ground on a hot August day in 1950. As with the XH-44 a half-dozen years earlier, there was no fanfare; the public as yet knew nothing about the new machine.

This first flight was somewhat restricted by an umbilical hose bringing fuel from a tank on the ground. As the craft would soon be carrying its own fuel, the company took the liberty of retouching the hose out of early Hornet photographs sent to various Pentagon offices to generate further support for Hiller's tip-powered flying crane proposals. Since the Army was clearly interested in flying cranes, photographs demonstrating successful tip-powered flight, albeit on a small scale, were certain to help the company effort.

Those who witnessed the testing of the HJ-1 knew that here was a new kind of helicopter. The gentility suggested by its diminutive size ended the moment it came to life: Flames streamed from its ramjets, growing shorter and disappearing as the rotor gathered speed with a businesslike roar. At dusk, dramatic blue fire ringed the craft. "At least one terrified motorist drove into [a] ditch when suddenly confronted with a low, fast-flying halo of brilliant blue flames," the Hiller company newspaper admitted.[3]

When the company finally unveiled the HJ-1 Hornet to the public on 27 February 1951, it received wide attention both in the aviation news media and in the general press. Three of these diminutive two-seaters were by then flying, two open and one with a fiberglass body; a fourth was built but not flown. The HJ-1 had a gross weight of 900 pounds and a height of just seven feet from the ground to the top of its twenty-three-foot-diameter rotor. Top speed was 80 mph, cruise was 70 mph, service ceiling was 11,000 feet, and initial rate of climb was a sprightly 1,100 fpm. The only drawback, thanks to its thirsty ramjets, was range: a fully loaded HJ-1 could travel only a little under forty miles.

In addition to a fuel gauge, therefore, the Hornet had a built-in low-fuel warning. Several minutes before its tanks ran dry, the aircraft would automatically throttle itself back to initiate a descent and alert the pilot to land soon. A short

standpipe with perforations to constrict fuel flow from the lowest reaches of the fuel tank produced this automatic power reduction. This safety feature would also be incorporated into the Hiller HOE/ H-32 series tip-powered helicopter described later in this chapter.

Because the tip mass of the ramjets added substantial inertia to the Hornet's rotor, making it a very effective flywheel, the rotor tended to maintain RPM despite slight changes in attitude or blade pitch. For this reason, the constant minor throttle adjustments required by most early helicopters were eliminated.

Better still, during forward flight each ramjet developed proportionately more power sweeping forward and less as it retreated. This self-throttling was simply the product of relative velocity; on the forward swing, the rotor's speed and the helicopter's forward airspeed combined to ram more air into the engine. This translated directly into more thrust. The engine on the retreating blade, meanwhile, received less ram air and produced less thrust. The result was a cyclical power boost just where needed to balance the load on the rotor head, thereby eliminating the need for a complex isolation system.

The HJ-1 was surprisingly stable for so small a craft because of its Rotormatic paddles and high-inertia rotor. The docile manners, however, ended at autorotation, an unpowered descent to landing practiced by helicopter pilots to prepare for the slim possibility of engine failure. Autorotation involves a controlled descent with the rotor in low pitch to keep it spinning. Near the ground, the pilot then increases blade pitch to trade the stored rotational energy for momentary lift. A soft landing results if the maneuver is performed properly.

Where conventional helicopters autorotate at a sobering 1,800 feet per minute or so, the Hiller Hornet plummeted at a terrifying 3,000 fpm because the gaping mouths of its dead ramjets retarded rotor windmilling. This aerodynamic braking was termed "cold drag." Nonetheless, however slowly it turned during autorotation, the massive rotor had *plenty* of accumulated kinetic energy left to trade for lift when the time came; one merely needed skill, nerve, and fast reflexes to know when to haul up on the collective pitch lever.

Hiller test pilot Bruce Jones was the first person to autorotate a tip-powered-rotor helicopter. Ground observers stood aghast as he hurtled downward in the HJ-1, came to a radical flare in the nick of time, and settled to the ground. With a mix of relief and anger, Hiller's nonpilot contracts manager ran up to the Hornet, shouting that the craft was not insured.

"Listen," the pilot replied hotly, steadying himself on rubbery legs. "I'm lucky to be alive! The aircraft was falling at 3,000 feet a minute and I was falling at 2,000, and I barely caught up with the controls to land the damn thing!"[4]

Jones, a veteran "hump" flier in the China-Burma-India theater of World War II and a former Bell Helicopters demonstration pilot, soon became the undisputed master of Hornet autorotations. An argument arose on the Hiller flightline one summer day in 1951 over what accuracy, if any, was possible during "deadstick" landings. Jones settled the issue once and for all by autorotating from 3,000 feet to land within fifty feet of dead center of the Hiller apron.

With no torque to counter, the Hornet dispensed with a tail rotor in favor of a simple airplane-style rudder, which was canted to take advantage of rotor downwash. Pedals were likewise eliminated; side-to-side movement of the collective lever worked the rudder to provide yaw control. An overhead cyclic stick provided lateral and longitudinal control as in the early model 360s. On the touchy subject of noise, Hiller publicity releases optimistically stated that "the Hornet's sound range compares favorably with that of a conventional-powered [*sic*] helicopter."[5]

The idea of a low-cost flying machine that could actually fit into an average-size garage briefly rekindled America's cherished dream of personal flying machines akin to cars. The Hornet certainly provided substantial raw material for such daydreams, having just two controls (cyclic and collective-cum-rudder) and fewer items on its instrument panel than the dashboard of the average automobile (tachometer, fuel flow gauge, airspeed indicator, altimeter, and starter button).

Unfortunately for this last gasp of the romantic vision of personal flying machines, the Korean War preempted plans to market the HJ-1. Viewing its rapidly expanding backlog of military helicopter orders, and an uncertain public demand for the HJ-1, Hiller Helicopters announced in September 1951 that plans for marketing a civil version of the Hornet had been indefinitely deferred.

Proponents of tip propulsion could at least take pleasure in the fact that the ramjets powering the little Hornet showed no hint of off-center burning despite the fairly constant 1,200 G's of centrifugal force to which they were subjected in flight. Since G loads increase as rotor diameter decreases, the tiny Hornet rotor offered convincing proof indeed.

Tip propulsion received another boost with the arrival in 1951 of Elbert Sargent, who had left McDonnell after heading the development of the XH-20 *Little Henry*. Imaginative and hard-working, Sargent had been aggressively courted by Hiller Helicopters; on his first visit, Stanley Hiller himself greeted the engineer at San Francisco International Airport to whisk him to Palo Alto by helicopter.

Sargent arrived at the Hiller plant to the sight and sound of free-flying ramjet helicopters skimming overhead. At Hiller he sensed a surprising commitment to ramjet and tip power, one rivaling that of McDonnell. "Hiller was then doing things we were not doing in Saint Louis," Sargent recalls. "The Hornet's flights at altitude and autorotations surpassed what we had achieved with *Little Henry*."[6] Joining the smaller company meant forsaking substantial seniority and the security of an industry giant, but Sargent did not hesitate to leave McDonnell and sign on as Hiller's new chief of propulsion.

Taking full advantage of the aviation press's fascination with the Hornet, the company continued to pursue its strategy of promoting flying cranes to exploit the great advantages tip power promised in large helicopters. For a time, this strategy appeared to be working; the military services spoke more and more frequently of heavy-lift helicopters.

Hiller had initially proposed a tip-powered "carryall" helicopter to the Navy in 1949, but nothing came of the effort. Early in 1951, therefore, the company proposed an intermediate-size "Aerial Carryall" or "Flying Truck" to the U.S. Army. With no transmission, shafting, or internal engine (except a small auxiliary power unit needed to start the main rotor), the vehicle offered an unencumbered, boxlike cargo compartment framed by an ultra-lightweight tubular structure, detachable cargo pods, and an assortment of hoists and hooks. Graceless and utterly utilitarian, it had precisely the capabilities an infantry general might wish for.

The U.S. Army Transportation Command responded with enthusiasm. Hiller's proposal looked good across a broad spectrum of uses: supply, field repair base, air ambulance, troop and cargo transport, mobile command post, mobile air station, and tanker were among the roles envisioned. The only reservation expressed by the Army centered on the Flying Truck's fuel consumption.

Ramjets, of course, were merely an interim expedient in a program whose ultimate goal was the use of much more efficient turbine engines. Fuel then being cheap and plentiful, the company believed the Army could live with ramjets since tactical use of the Flying Truck on battle fronts did not require much range. At a projected gross weight of eight tons, the vehicle as proposed could fly for thirty minutes with a load of 9,000 pounds; adding sufficient fuel to remain aloft ninety minutes reduced useful load to 4,725 pounds.

Because the Army was then still constrained to acquire its aircraft through other services, primarily the U.S. Air Force, Hiller realized that steps were needed to make the Flying Truck palatable to that service as well. First, the company strengthened its proposal with added technical data. Second, it reduced the vehicle's payload to 8,000 pounds in order to give it smoother lines more in keeping with the Air Force's sleek postwar look. Third, Hiller divided the program into a stepped development rather than an all-or-nothing procurement; presented as a research program, phase one of Flying Truck development might be more acceptable to the Air Force.

After receiving the proposal, the Air Force instructed Hiller to submit details of the craft's proposed large-diameter rotor system for its review. A stumbling block now arose when the USAF refused to recognize the Palo Alto company as an engine manufacturer. As a result, Hiller was advised to team up with the Marquardt Corporation of Van Nuys, California, a builder of rockets and ramjets. If it did not, the Air Force would not fund Hiller development of tip-powered helicopters for the Army.

Despite a personal friendship between Stan Hiller and Roy Marquardt, the other California company was as unenthusiastic as Hiller Helicopters about the association. Roy Marquardt had formed his company in 1944 specifically to pursue jet-propelled helicopter research, and his company paralleled Hiller's in many ways, although generally with less success. Like Hiller, Marquardt had pursued development of a coaxial helicopter (never built), had conducted tip-propulsion studies with pulse jets and ramjets, had designed a pressure-jet rotor, and had even undertaken construction in 1947 of a two-place pulse jet–powered helicopter.

Even as Hiller and Marquardt worked out the details of such an association, the Air Force killed the Flying Truck program. In a carefully worded response, the USAF informed the Army that the latter service had no need of large helicopters. The statement—which ignored the vehicle's obvious applicability to Army field operations—was patently absurd.

Hiller's Flying Truck was partly the victim of ineffectual procurement, for the Army's civilian technical experts at Fort Eustis, Virginia, had failed to provide the convincing hard technical support necessary for passage of such a program. The Air Force's response suggested, however, that the Flying Truck had also fallen prey to ongoing wrangling between an Air Force that jealously defended its hold on airpower, and an Army that found itself crippled by the Key West Accord. By canceling the Flying Truck, the USAF—probably perceiving in any resurgence of Army aviation a threat to its own missions and goals—had simply acted in its own self-interest.

Having been denied meaningful airpower of its own under the 1947 reorganization, the Army was in theory supposed to call upon the Air Force to make up the lack. Unfortunately, the USAF was rarely there when the Army needed it; a postwar focus on supersonic jet interceptors and long-range strategic bombers left the Air Force poorly equipped to provide ground support. It was clear that despite Key West rhetoric, the USAF had better things to do than to provide air cover for the Army.

Forgotten amid the politics was one of World War II's clearest lessons: close air support works best when controlled directly by field commanders. If instead it must be "requested" from elsewhere, the response is inevitably less satisfactory. More than one battle has been lost to second-guessing and to requests for additional information by air commanders unacquainted with real-time battlefield requirements.

If the Navy could have a full air force of its own, Army personnel wondered, why couldn't the nation's field forces have a broad slate of tactical and logistical air vehicles at their disposal? The Air Force was the obvious villain, of course, but the truth lay elsewhere. After all, the USAF had not drafted the Key West Accord of 1948.

In fact, the Army had only itself to blame for its current troubles. It had failed to stand up for Army aviation when the Key West agreement was signed between the joint chiefs of staff. Wanting little to do with air power (for reasons discussed in the preceding chapter), Army leaders absolved themselves at that key juncture of dealing with the issue; if the Air Force wanted it, the Army's leadership felt, let them have it.

Had Army leadership chosen to address the issue of air power, to consider realistically Army aviation requirements over the coming decades, the Air Force would not have succeeded in staking so comprehensive a claim. In the absence of protest, however, the Air Force defined for itself

at Key West a role so broad as to all but preempt a meaningful aviation program for the Army. Thus, the outdated 1942 "organic aviation" agreement, which made light "grasshopper" airplanes available to ground commanders, was extended by default in 1948.

By willingly ceding aviation to the Air Force, the Army also deprived itself of a mechanism for direct procurement of military aircraft. As a consequence, it would have to obtain its aircraft either through the Air Force or the Navy. The only other option available to it was to buy civil aircraft ill-suited to military use in what became known as "off-the-shelf" procurement. Had the Army still been able to pursue its own procurements in the 1950s, of course, the Air Force would not have been in a position to cancel the Hiller Flying Truck and other programs.

The Navy—which maintained its own air arm and therefore also frequently grappled with the Air Force over roles and missions—also took a serious look at heavy-lift tip-powered helicopters. The most vulnerable time for any ship at sea is when it is taking on provisions; to be attacked while receiving supplies from a tender is every Naval commander's worst nightmare. Flying cranes could significantly reduce this vulnerability by shuttling supplies on an ongoing basis, thereby eliminating the need for ships to huddle together in the water.

Among those within the Navy who recognized the need for such a machine was Coast Guard Captain Richard L. Henson. Improbable as it might sound, Henson had been posted to the Navy's requirements desk in Washington because he was one of the few authorities on helicopter operations the Navy could muster after World War II. Henson had, in fact, already played a role in helicopter history.

Although development of the Sikorsky R-4 during World War II had been sponsored by the U.S. Army Air Forces, the first production R-4s went instead to the U.S. Navy and Coast Guard, and to the British. Captain Henson, one of the few outspoken visionaries in the American camp who saw the helicopter's potential, pushed to acquire R-4s for coastal submarine patrol. A wartime congressional committee, created to oversee and investigate the national defense program, agreed with him. Known popularly as the Truman Committee after its chairman, Senator Harry S. Truman, this influential body decreed that the armed services must make use of this valuable new form of flight. The Army finally put R-4s of its own into service during the last year of the war, using them in the China-Burma-India theater of operations.

Hiller met with Henson in 1950 and found a kindred spirit who shared his belief in the value of heavy vertical-lift aircraft. Months of work between their Washington offices produced a USN requirement in June 1951 for a "Class HC" heavy lifter, to which Hiller responded with a proposal for a tip-powered collapsible helicopter. This huge machine, when folded, would fit in the hangar deck of an aircraft carrier and could go up its flight-deck elevator. Yet it was big enough, when unfolded, to lift crippled aircraft off the deck or to resupply capital ships while under way.

As proposed, the Hiller HC Cargo Unloader was a tubular structure some-how suggestive of a praying mantis, topped by a rotor fully a hundred feet across. At an all-up gross weight of 26.3 tons, it had an estimated maximum speed of 111 knots (128 mph) with a rate of climb of over 3,000 fpm, and it could reach a ceiling of 16,000 feet. In the proposal, Hiller listed three power systems. The first was a flat, twin-chambered ramjet with multiple nozzles and burners, similar to those used on the Hornet. The second was an advanced intermittent-flow sonic engine, which would appear in the late 1950s as the Hiller "Pulse Reactor." The third power configuration employed two turbojet engines mounted side-by-side on each of the two blade tips. This last option would have been first but for lack of interest among jet engine manufacturers, which, in turn, meant that the Hiller Cargo Unloader proposal would live or die on the merits of ramjet power alone.

Submissions from elsewhere in the helicopter and aircraft industries included a number of conventional helicopters and a pressure-jet design from McDonnell. At first Hiller was confident that its proposal would win, since it had generated the requirement and fostered the competition, but it soon became clear that neither Hiller nor any helicopter manufacturer had a hope of winning the Cargo Unloader contract. The Navy and Department of Defense were not willing to look any farther afield than McDonnell, the well-entrenched fixed-wing manufacturer they knew from long association.

More was at work here than the pervasive misconception that a small company could not build a large aircraft. Rightly or wrongly, the Pentagon's relationships with its suppliers was such that it effectively barred entry to newcomers when major aviation contracts were at stake; the Navy and Air Force each had its fixed suppliers, with some overlap of course. If ready market access is indeed an underpinning of the free enterprise system, these rather incestuous alliances—which did not necessarily run counter to the national interest—may well have contributed to President Dwight Eisenhower's prophetic warning about the military-industrial complex as he left office in 1961.

This experience underscored the parallel plight of the Army and the helicopter industry which supplied it; both held second-class status. Hiller, Bell, Sikorsky and Vertol responded by redoubling their efforts at education, and by supporting at every turn the young Army "Turks" whose ardent advocacy of the helicopter often fell on deaf ears at the top. Hiller— the "Army's company" in the sense that it and postwar Army aviation were growing up together—inevitably took the lead in this process.

The winner of the Navy's Cargo Unloader requirement turned out to be McDonnell in St. Louis, a builder of Navy jet fighter planes. Guided by Friedrich Doblhoff, who had immigrated to the United States after World War II, McDonnell pursued development of a pressure-jet rotor. McDonnell's approach to tip propulsion was one already abandoned by Hiller as fraught with compromise. Predictably, the rotor proved disappointing on the teststand, and the project Hiller had worked so hard to engender was canceled.

Hiller proposed the construction of

an evaluation quantity of Hornets to the Navy early in 1952. If the flying crane was out for the time being, acquainting the Navy with ramjets and tip power could only work in Hiller's favor in the future. The company's commitment to so promising a line of research remained firm.

Spurred by a Marine Corps request for an ultralight flying vehicle, the Navy responded positively to Hiller's proposal. By summer, a fixed price contract had been negotiated for delivery of five units. Three would go to the Navy as the HOE-1. Having been impressed by the simplicity of the original HJ-1, the Army would then take the remaining two under the designation YH-32. At the end of 1954, the Army ordered a dozen more Hornets, and Hiller's own test and demonstration requirements brought the grand total of second-generation Hornets to twenty-five, including the three ULV *Sally Rand* gunships described below. It was the first production run of tip-jet-powered helicopters in history and the first procurement of such vehicles by U.S. military services.[7]

Coming only a year after the rift between the Navy and Hiller (caused by the Convair contingent, since departed from Palo Alto), the order for HOE-1s might at first glance seem to belie hard feelings on the part of Navy procurement officials. The small order for test and evaluation machines, however, came from a different branch with its own procurement desk. When it came to operational aircraft, the grudge was still in place.

Although the new military helicopter shared the name and designation of the three original HJ-1 Hornets, it was in fact an all-new machine with no commonality. Instead of wheels, it had lightweight skids. Gone too was the rudder worked by moving the collective lever from side to side; the new HJ-1 had rudder pedals controlling a tiny single-blade tail rotor (the rotor and pedals were reinstated for commonality with other military helicopters). While not needed to offset torque, the tail rotor—which provided crisper yaw control than did the earlier Hornet's rudder—helped during autorotation and permitted rapid sideways flight as required by increasingly stringent military control requirements.

The HOE/H-32 was a trim machine with perky lines that might just as easily have sprung from Walt Disney's drawing board as from the Hiller team's. In fact, it was designed by both Bob Anderson and vice-president of engineering James B. Edwards, who had come to Hiller in January 1952 from Douglas Aircraft where he had been project engineer on the famous DC-4 and DC-6 airliners (Edwards would return to Douglas late in 1953 and fulfill the same function on the DC-7).

Unfortunately, as often happens with military involvement in a previously private venture, the HJ-1 suffered a growth in size and weight. A larger cockpit, a fiberglass body and tail boom (the first structural use of fiberglass in aircraft construction), and other changes raised the empty weight from the original Hornet's 356 pounds to 536 pounds, and the gross weight climbed to 1,080 pounds. As a result, the service ceiling fell drastically from 11,000 to 6,900 feet. Even with fifty-two gallons of fuel, the craft's range shrank from forty to twenty-eight miles, its maximum powered endurance at econ-

omy cruise being roughly thirty minutes. The decreased performance frustrated the Hiller team, which felt that the HJ-1 had evolved away from the original concept of a truly simple helicopter. Worse still, the joint military program was worked over and over by the Army and Navy with so many extracontractual changes that— including the dual certification programs described below—it eventually consumed more than a million dollars of Hiller resources.

Even so, 1953 was a good year for Hiller Helicopters; its net income after taxes was a healthy $247,637. Commercial sales of the Model 12 climbed to 20 percent of the company's total business after civil production resumed early that year, and the commercial market continued to grow steadily. With new construction complete, total plant space stood at 146,000 square feet and the employment roster had risen to 550.

The first of the HOE/H-32 series flew in September 1953, with deliveries to commence the following spring. The services did not receive them until the end of 1954, however, because these machines had been procured on a "certification specification" basis rather than on the standard "mil. spec." basis, and civil certification of the helicopter and its engine would take time, as both were new to the experience of the Civil Aeronautics Administration (predecessor to today's Federal Aviation Administration).

The 8RJ2B ramjet engine was a refined and uprated version of the unit Hiller had developed in 1949. Now 8 inches in diameter and weighing 12.7 pounds, it produced the equivalent of 45-

horsepower. It was manufactured by Ryan in San Diego under license from Hiller and was made out of Inconel X, a high-nickel alloy also used in the Mach 6 North American X-15 research plane owing to its lightness and great resistance to heat. Because Inconel X corrodes on contact with lead, then commonly found in automotive gasoline which was a likely fuel for this engine, the engine's interior was coated with a protective ceramic material.

By August, the 8RJ2B had logged 559 hours in the air, 2,104 hours on the whirl-stand, and 1,545 hours in free airstream static tests. Its early technical troubles had been completely solved, even the once-nagging problem of flameouts. If flameouts should occur, the engine now reignited itself so quickly that the pilot never suspected he had experienced the problem. Another selling point was the remarkable portability and simplicity of the 8RJ2B; for example, an untrained person could change a Hornet's engine in just three minutes with nothing more than a screwdriver.

Ramjet testing on the ground included static duration runs, which were a very sore point with residents of Belle Haven and East Palo Alto. One test in March 1953 lasted 200 hours, while another the following February ran for 150 hours. At night when all was otherwise still, moreover, an inversion would often form over the entire San Francisco Bay Area causing the "bam! bam! bam!" of the whirling ramjets to skip over much of the local area and bounce squarely into the fashionable Atherton–Menlo Park neighborhoods. Needless to say, it was

not welcome. Nor could the company president himself escape it; the disagreeable noise often greeted Hiller when he returned home to Atherton at night.

Harried residents telephoning the plant at Palo Alto to complain found sympathetic listeners there, many of whom yielded to the temptation to suggest that the sound "must be coming from the Navy at Moffett Field."[8] Fortunately, the problem was significantly reduced in the spring of 1954 by construction of a circular barrier eighteen feet high and forty feet in diameter which was designed to muffle jet-engine noise. Since the structure could not entirely encircle the facility without depriving it of sufficient air, however, the side facing the bay was left open. The necessity of building the barrier hinted at the seriousness of the tip-engine noise problem; in a world increasingly intolerant of aircraft noise, the issue was a growing obstacle to realization of Hiller Helicopters' vision of tip-turbine flying cranes.

During the last days of ramjet certification in 1954, a series of overspeed runs was conducted on the whirlstand. At peak rpm, when the tip jet was subjected to as much as 14,000 Gs (boosting its "weight" to some 178,000 pounds), supporting bolts sheared and the 8RJ2B shot away through protective walls, acoustical barriers, and property fences before coming to rest some 500 feet from the test site. The teststand also departed the area, flying off toward San Francisco Bay. It was later recovered from nearby mud flats. This was the only known structural failure of a Hiller tip-power rotor; the test far exceeded expectations and

*J*oined by Hiller's bright yellow
prototype, ten green Army YH-32s
await delivery. The Army eventually
received fourteen YH-32s.

overwhelmingly satisfied the stringent certification requirements.

On 28 October 1954, the Civil Aeronautics Administration awarded Hiller's 8RJ2B engine Type Certificate No. 280, officially approving it for commercial production and sale should Hiller so desire. But further pioneering developments in power plant technology very soon overshadowed this unit, and Hiller moved beyond the ramjet. Nonetheless, as the first American-designed and manufactured jet engine to be approved for production, the Hiller 8RJ2B represents a milestone in aviation history.

Unfortunately, parallel certification for the Hornet itself was not granted. The reason was the cold-drag problem associated with autorotation, as described above in the earlier HJ-1. The new military Hornets descended steeply at almost 3,500 fpm, but their massive rotors stored so much energy that landings were simple after one became accustomed—if one ever could—to the high sink rate. Hiller test pilot and marketing executive Robert Boughton found that whereas one would begin to flare fifty to sixty feet above the ground in a normal helicopter, the Hornet demanded that one begin pulling up on the collective lever a full two to three hundred feet off the ground. Enough inertia was stored in the tip engines that the pilot could touch down, rise into the air again, and land a second time.

A solution to the unacceptably high sink rate was proposed to the military during development of the H-32 and HOE. The company suggested that the flameholders in the mouths of the ramjets be modified to function like controllable shutters. During autorotation, they could simply rotate shut to close off airflow through the engine and thus greatly reduce cold drag.

Flameouts had by now been all but eliminated, and even if one engine failed, the Hornet could be flown some distance to a safe landing, although it could not maintain altitude. An automatic low-fuel power reduction—described earlier in this chapter—further enhanced safety by alerting the pilot to land while sufficient fuel remained. Still, with range so limited and the possibility of fuel starvation so great, flameholder shutters were clearly a desirable feature.

The military declined because its strict acceptance standards made no provision for such devices. Without them, the Hornet's autorotation proved unacceptable to the CAA, which otherwise found the diminutive craft satisfactory. Civil certification was accordingly denied. Failure to achieve this production license removed any possibility of the Hornet's reaching the private market, although it is doubtful that Hiller would have chosen to market a civil version in any event.

What was it like to fly the Hiller HOE-1/YH-32? Starting it was easy, if not instantaneous, since a small electric motor first had to spin the rotor up to 150 rpm, or one-third its operating speed. Fuel pressure was then built up, fuel flow valves were opened, and the starter button was depressed to fire a spark plug in each ramjet. Ninety seconds later, the Hornet's rotor reached 450–500 rpm— and away it flew. Pilots who had the chance to try it out reported generally pleasant and forgiving characteristics.

All this activity, meanwhile, engendered new flying crane stirrings within the Army, as Hiller had hoped. Major General Frank S. Besson, then head of the Army Transportation Corps, requested a design study from Hiller for a huge tip-powered helicopter with a two-hundred-foot rotor. This initiative—which failed to progress beyond the paper stage—was known as "BARC" for "Besson's Airborne Railhead Crane." Informally and somewhat humorously, it was also interpreted to mean "Besson's Ark."

By the time the military services ordered their Hornets, Hiller had taken a ramjet and added moving parts to develop two new types of pulse jets, the "rotafire" and "rotamonic" units of 1952. Development of both was prompted in part by the "cold drag" penalty of the ramjet, and in part because—being essentially low-order turbojets—these remarkable new power plants substantially narrowed the gap toward true tip-turbine propulsion. John B. Nichols, Elbert Sargent, and Ray Lockwood led this engineering effort.

Hiller's rotafire engine had a rotating valve disc at its inlet and another at its exhaust. The two were connected by a central shaft. Bracketing the combustion chamber, which was divided longitudinally into ten separate cells, these discs—functioning much like movie projector shutters—served as valves to produce the jet equivalent of a four-cycle piston engine. With both valves open, scavenge air passed through the cell to flush exhaust gasses and bring in fresh air and fuel. Then both ends of the cell closed for constant-volume combustion, producing a steep pressure rise. The exhaust valve then opened to produce thrust aft,

after which the front valve also opened to start the cycle again. With the ten combustion cells firing sequentially, the rotafire ran smoothly and produced a regular net thrust.

The simpler rotamonic dispensed with the rear rotating valve and had a single combustion chamber. By harmonically inducing the desired engine operating frequency, its inlet valve achieved pulse-jet operation without the need of a long tail pipe. In its functioning, therefore, the rotamonic engine also belonged to the sonic engine family, which was the next phase of Hiller power-plant development.

Sonic engines are pulse jets with resonant combustors (in effect, harmonically tuned tail pipes) instead of mechanical valving to induce pulsation. They have no flapping valves or shutters to be hindered by centrifugal force when the engine is used for tip propulsion. With multiple tail pipes, sonic engines are also shorter and thus better suited to the tip environment. While still quite thirsty by piston engine standards, sonic engines are 40 to 50 percent more fuel efficient than are ramjets. They are also very loud. Hiller engineers played with, but did not pursue, the intriguing idea of tuning them so that most of their noise would fall above the range of human hearing.

To underwrite the expense of testing, Hiller used its successful ground evaluation of these unusual power plants as the basis for proposal to the U.S. Army that it support further development. Funding was not forthcoming, however, and none of these engines was ever flown.

Behind the scenes, the company continued to expand. On the business front,

Certification of the Hiller 8RJ2B ramjet, the first American-designed and built jet engine of any kind to be approved for production, is granted on 28 October 1954. Marking the historic event are (l-r) chief engineer Robert Wagner, Kenneth Beymer and Russell van Note of the CAA, chief of propulsion Elbert R. Sargent, project engineer Harvey Holm, and experimental shop supervisor Edward Bennett.

Hiller Helicopters now had a new executive vice-president and general manager. Arriving in the spring of 1954, Edward T. Bolton brought management skills honed during years of singular service with airlines around the world. The British-born executive, also named a director of the company, replaced William C. Jordan, the former Curtiss-Wright Corporation head, who left the post after one year.

When in the spring of 1952 Hiller Helicopters received the first contract ever issued for study of a rotary-wing gun platform, the company came up with a ramjet-powered craft rugged and simple enough to "live with the troops."[9] Code named LANAR, the proposed "triphibian" vehicle—LANAR was at home on land, water, and in the air—resembled a futuristic jeep topped with both a foldable rotor and a formidable assortment of weaponry. Nothing came of this effort except an invitation to submit another proposal under the project name ASTRON, this time for an unmanned aerial weapons platform. Hiller responded with a rather far-fetched armored vehicle resembling an inverted GI helmet topped by a ramjet rotor. Wire-guided by hand controls, this inverted tank would brave withering fire to deliver rockets and other ordnance.

To an Army senior staff ever mindful of the Key West Accord, these patently offensive aerial weapons had no place in Army planning, so they never got past the Deputy Chief of Staff. LANAR and ASTRON had in fact been commissioned by the Detroit Arsenal rather than by Hiller's usual Army customers. This latter camp successfully killed the projects before they could raise a red flag elsewhere in the Pentagon.

Army field commanders who wanted such weapons in their arsenal were close to prevailing, however, as Key West restrictions continued to ease. By 1955, in fact, Hiller would receive the first contract ever awarded in the United States for construction of an armed helicopter. Today largely forgotten, the resulting craft—a last incarnation of the HOE/H-32 Hornet series—was designated the Hiller YH-32A ULV. Fostered by General James Gavin, a premier advocate of air support for Army Field Forces, this Hiller minigunship marks a major milestone in the rebirth of Army aviation.

Because it was "stripped to the bare essentials," the ULV (ultralight vehicle) was nicknamed *Sally Rand* after the dancer whose nude performances had enlivened Chicago's Century of Progress Exhibition in 1933. Three YH-32As were built and tested in 1957 at Fort Rucker, Alabama, where they successfully carried and employed combinations of rockets, wire-guided missiles, a 75-mm recoilless cannon, land-mine detectors, and other equipment. The new craft featured twin tails, because recoilless cannons discharge gasses rearward to counteract their recoil when fired. Simplicity dictated a return to canted rudders instead of a tail rotor. *Sally* followed the troops in a tarpaulin-covered trailer that housed spare parts, refueling equipment, and ordnance. With its side panels folded down, the trailer became a launch platform.

Under a separate contract, a modified ULV was tested at an abandoned airstrip in central California to determine its

The Army's first contract for armed helicopters produced three Hiller YH-32A ULVs (ultralight vehicles) in 1955. Shown on a trailer with its sides folded down to form a launch platform, the ULV—which incorporated a Hornet rotor and systems— successfully carried and fired wire-guided missiles, rockets, and a 75-mm recoilless cannon.

vulnerability to enemy action. Although diminutive dimensions made it a difficult target to hit, the craft's size and limited range clearly rendered it unsuitable for operational use. As a proof-of-concept vehicle, however, the YH-32A ULV was successful, paving the way for the U.S. Army's heavy commitment to helicopter firepower during the Vietnam War.

The Hiller company's ongoing tip-power research and its parametric studies of flying cranes, performed under military contract, laid the groundwork for practical application of tip propulsion. Dramatic success in the area of flying cranes was within easy reach but for want of the official support Hiller continued to seek. In the meantime, testing continued on a smaller scale as the company explored new approaches to the fuel consumption problem.

In a true helicopter, the powered rotor corresponds to both an airplane's wing, which provides lift, and its propeller, which provides thrust. The windmilling rotor of an autogyro, in contrast, provides only lift; the thrust is supplied separately by an airplane-style propeller. Hiller engineers reasoned that a hybrid machine—half helicopter and half autogyro—would offer the best of both worlds: Ramjets would be used for vertical operations and hovering, of which autogyros are not capable, but in flight the tip engines would be shut down and the craft would fly like a conventional autogyro.

Called Autogyro 1A or Model 1013, this Hiller test vehicle of 1953 was in fact a "convertiplane" consisting of a modified HJ-1 (a fourth early Hornet, which had not been completed) equipped with a 65-hp McCulloch four-cylinder aircraft engine driving a tractor propeller. Pilot Bruce Jones flew this experimental craft early that year, but did not attempt a transition in flight between forms of propulsion because—like Hornets during autorotation—the Autogyro 1A suffered badly in horizontal flight from the cold drag of its windmilling ramjets. It was planned that Hiller's next convertiplane would use the new rotafire engine to get around the problem.

Development began, meanwhile, of a folding rotor like that proposed by Hiller for LANAR. Stemming from a 1953 Air Force contract (the first ever issued for a "stowable rotor," an idea evaluated by many manufacturers over the years), this Hiller effort studied the feasibility of equipping conventional airplanes with rotors. Housed internally during conventional high-speed flight, this rotor would extend for helicopter-style hovering and landings. By early 1956, development had reached the point where a 25-foot-diameter unit (the industry's first full-scale, working, stowable rotor) was ready for testing in NACA Langley's full-scale wind tunnel under the sponsorship of the USAF's Air Development Center at Wright-Patterson Air Force Base.[10] Wind tunnel evaluation of this rotor concluded the contract, and the military shelved the concept.

That Hiller—which had not initiated the project—was by now well versed in the ways of military R&D was clear from its ability to snatch this contract away from a broad field of aerospace bidders. Company hopes for further testing, and perhaps military application, of Hiller stowable rotors were not fulfilled because of a general shift toward other approaches to achieving VTOL flight.

Central Intelligence Agency interest in obtaining superquiet aircraft preempted plans for using rotafire engines in Hiller's continuing convertiplane program. Modified at Hiller Plant 2 in Redwood City, California, the Autogyro 1A emerged as Autogyro 2, or Model 1013A, in 1954. In addition to a 125-hp Lycoming engine salvaged from one of the coaxial Commuters, the new craft was powered by tiny hydrogen-peroxide tip rockets an inch thick. Hiller engineers patterned these 35-pound-thrust engines after similar units which had been developed by other companies then experimenting with hydrogen-peroxide rocket propulsion.

In contrast to the pulse jets and ramjets that had assaulted the ears of Hiller employees for so long, Autogyro 2 was startlingly quiet in hovering flight. The tip rockets produced a muted noise reminiscent of a quiet steam engine, while the well-muffled Lycoming itself was scarcely audible at idle. The heavy weights at the blade tips combined with the low-drag rockets to produce a rotor whose engine-out performance has seldom if ever been equalled. A pilot could hover at thirty feet, cut power, and take as much time as was wanted in a leisurely descent before running out of rotor inertia. Better still, the problem of cold drag which had afflicted the Hornet helicopter did not exist here.

This project came to an abrupt and tragic halt in 1955 when a test pilot ruptured a fuel line in a hard landing, causing a small fire. The pilot—who was on contract to the project and was not a member of Hiller's flight test department—was unhurt and would have been all right had not an excited assistant grabbed what he thought was a large jug of water and doused him with its contents. A moment later the assistant realized he had used the hydrogen-peroxide supply bottle, but by then it was too late: the unfortunate test pilot was massively and fatally burned.

Although the promising hybrid concept of Autogyro 2 might well have found application, all work with hydrogen peroxide was henceforth abandoned by Hiller Helicopters. It is a measure of the character of the company that it gave up autogyro and convertiplane research even though the fatality was attributable to a ground accident and not to aircraft failure. In fact, no one would be killed or even seriously injured as a direct result of flight testing during the company's quarter century of aviation activity.

Free steam had also been considered by Hiller but was not tested in flight. William J. Besler, the dean of steam power, joined the Hiller team assembled for this effort. A Travel Air biplane equipped with a Besler steam engine had made aviation's first manned steam-powered airplane flight in Oakland in April 1933. In more recent years, Besler had been associated with the Doble Company (also known as Doble Detroit), which built steam-powered cars.

A related Hiller tip-power project was the Model 14 captive observation helicopter. This simple tethered research platform was powered by compressed air supplied from the ground.

At the American Helicopter Society's Ninth Annual Forum in 1953, Hiller engineer John Nichols expressed his company's conviction that no form of power would ultimately be right for ultra-large helicopters except blade-mounted turbine engines. Seven years later, at the Society's Sixteenth Annual National Forum in Washington, D.C., Nichols in a perhaps optimistic presentation gave the following description of subsequent progress in the quest for tip propulsion:

The advancements since 1953 in the propulsion industry have been beyond our wildest dreams, to the point where engine weights have been reduced to practically insignificant values and specific fuel consumptions reduced well below those which we originally specified. With the marked reduction in power plant weights, many of the fundamental technical problems have been so reduced in importance as to become completely innocuous. The tip turbojet concept has for all practical purposes been reduced from an advanced engineering venture into one of a practically routine nature.[11]

In 1955, Hiller had submitted to the military a performance study of various tip-turbojet helicopter configurations, which in turn generated Army and Navy contracts for the company, calling for parametric design studies of flying cranes with gross weights of up to 150,000 pounds. By 1958, armed with the results of these and earlier studies as well as thousands of hours of actual tip-propulsion experience, Hiller had a commanding lead when the Army finally solicited heavy-lift helicopter proposals from the industry. At the time of Nichols's presentation in May 1960, prospects seemed at their brightest for tip-turbine flying cranes.

Each manufacturer had responded with its own idea of what a flying crane should be. Sikorsky and Vertol, for example, both proposed scaled-up conventional helicopters. Hughes, disappointed with the failure of its XH-17 cold-cycle pressure-jet flying crane, now proposed a hot-cycle machine.

After reviewing the various submittals, the Army now issued a formal request for proposals (RFP) for a tip-turbine-powered flying crane in the Hiller mold. This time the service wanted more than theoretical data; the RFP initiated a three-phase program which, if successful, would culminate in a full-scale flying prototype in the 1960s. With such intriguing and potentially lucrative possibilities on the horizon, many manufacturers responded to the request.

The Army as a whole recognized Hiller's lead in the field of tip propulsion, but its Transportation Research and Engineering Command (TRECOM)—until very recently known as the Transportation Research and Development Command (TRADCOM)—favored the Hughes proposal. Based at Fort Eustis, Virginia, TRECOM was often derisively referred to as "Fort Useless" by industry and military personnel alike because its civilian technical advisors so often failed to provide the Army with the hard technical support it needed to defend its procurement efforts. The effect of TRECOM's preference for a hot-cycle approach was to draw out an already slow procurement effort.

Although not without precedent, one major Army decision dismayed Hiller Aircraft: the company's research data and design work were to be submitted openly to the entire aviation industry. The infor-

A model of the Hiller-Continental flying crane "flies" in a wind tunnel in the early 1960s. Winner of the Army's industrywide heavy-lift helicopter competition of the early 1960s, this program was canceled before a prototype could be constructed.

mation to be shared had been generated under military contract and was not proprietary, but many observers nevertheless felt the decision to be unfair.

Meanwhile, lacking immediate funds for company-financed tests on the flying-crane scale, Hiller exercised a valuable option not previously available to it. Williams Research Corporation in Michigan had recently developed a tiny turbojet engine just 15 inches long and 10 inches in diameter as a power plant for military target drones. Weighing 23 pounds and producing 83 pounds of static thrust, the Williams WR2-1 turbojet was the ancestor of today's cruise missile engines. Hiller and Williams reached an agreement in the fall of 1961, and by the following February the first turbojet ever mounted on a rotor blade was being whirled at Palo Alto.

These whirlstand tests began quite conservatively because tip engines are subjected to much higher G loads and gyroscopic forces by small-diameter rotors than by large ones. Word that a stock WR2-1 had run without difficulty at 140 G's, and that Hiller was now preparing to test a tip-modified version at 1,200 G's, gained timely new support for the Palo Alto company because, except for its size, the WR2-1 was similar to the Continental engine now slated for use on Hiller's full-size flying crane rotor.

Hiller had recently joined forces with the Continental Motors Corporation, whose Aircraft Engine Division produced the J69, a French-designed centrifugal-flow turbojet developing 1,700 pounds of thrust. Supporting this joint effort, Continental had already begun modification

of a power plant for tip use under the designation J69-T29.

The Hiller-Continental team proposed a three-phase program to the Army: Phase I would cover design studies at Hiller and development of the Continental J69-T29. Phase II called for construction of both the rotor system and engine, to be whirl-tested for a minimum of fifty hours. Phase III would witness the construction and testing of an actual Hiller flying crane. The proposed machine was designed to transport a twelve-ton payload fifty nautical miles at a speed of sixty to one hundred knots. The engines on its huge rotor would be subjected continuously to an estimated 235 G's.

Predictably, in the intense competition, other companies pointed to Hiller Aircraft's lack of experience in the construction of large aircraft. The latter issue was, of course, a political quagmire, for were Hiller to win the contract, Sikorsky or Vertol—America's traditional manufacturers of large helicopters—would lose what many considered to be a proprietary plum. As neither of these companies had ever pursued tip-propulsion research, however, it was hard to argue that anyone but Hiller should build the tip-turbojet flying crane.

For its part, Hiller observed that it was the third-largest supplier of helicopters in the free world, and that it had logged 6,000 hours of combined tip-propulsion whirl-test and flight experience, and that it indeed had large aircraft experience, having built the X-18 and part of the XC-142A (see chapter 5). Finally, Hiller pointed out that it was constructing at

Moffett Field the largest and most powerful dynamic teststand in the United States. Intended for the XC-142A, this valuable facility could be inexpensively adapted to use for flying crane development.

The Hiller-Continental team was awarded the Phase I contract for heavy-lift rotor development in the early 1960s. Hiller began designing a full-scale turbojet test rotor. At this juncture, it was learned that Hughes was estimating the end performance of its hot-cycle flying crane on the basis of new-generation high-performance engines only now in the early stages of development. This Hughes ploy—a well-known tactic the industry calls using "rubber engines"—suddenly placed the Hiller flying crane at an extreme disadvantage: lacking comparable power-plant technology as a baseline, any comparison of performance between these programs would misleadingly favor the Hughes design.

Hiller found itself with little recourse. Continental was unwilling to commit to development of a new jet engine to even up the odds, and Fort Eustis personnel refused to permit Hiller to employ other manufacturers' new-generation engine data as Hughes was doing. TRECOM insisted—as it had every right to do—that Hiller compete on the basis of its original agreement.

In February 1963, Army Chief of Research and Development Dwight Beach appeared before the House Armed Services Committee to justify fiscal year 1964 budgets. Deep in his testimony, General Beach announced plans to evaluate "the Hiller Aircraft concept . . . of

driving rotors with the thrust developed by turbojet engines mounted on the ends of rotor blades."[12] It came as all the more of a surprise to Hiller Aircraft, therefore, when the Army canceled the Hiller-Continental effort in the second quarter of 1965.

Plagued by internal dissent, under fire from the USAF for violation of Key West provisions, and undermined by a civilian technical staff at odds with the service it was supposed to support, the program wound inexorably to a halt. After nearly two decades of dedication to the concept, Hiller's flying crane program appeared to be over.

TRECOM, meanwhile, had funded the hot-cycle project Hughes had originally proposed to the Army. Flown in November 1964, the Hughes XV-9A research prototype (which used exhaust ducted from two General Electric T64 turbine engines) proved unsuccessful and the project was abandoned in 1969.

Nonetheless, the hot-cycle pressure-jet rotor idea (dismissed by Hiller in 1950 as inherently less efficient than tip turbines) holds a perennial fascination for engineers and it is a recurring theme in aviation to this day. New hot-cycle efforts appear periodically, are hailed as major and "new" breakthroughs, and are built, tested, and quietly laid to rest again.

Stanley Hiller's criterion for measuring his own business success is always how well he addresses his responsibility to those who invest in him. His company's substantial commitment to tip propulsion over time was never so great that it curbed the overall trend of increasing profitability. This cancellation was far from critical, therefore, and it was written off as just another research-and-development outlay among many. Such is the nature of aviation manufacture that few R&D efforts ever lead to production.

The end of the Hiller-Continental heavy-lift effort took little personal toll on Hiller despite his faith in the tip-engine flying crane concept. At this stage in his life, the setback—amid much productive activity as described in the next chapter—was received philosophically. "By that time," the company president reflected, "I simply did not look upon one loss as all that important."[13]

A 1965 conversation between Stanley Hiller and Wernher von Braun briefly revived hopes that the Hiller company might have an opportunity to build a tip-powered helicopter larger than any it had ever proposed. By this time concerned with spacecraft as well as aircraft (because of the formation of Fairchild Hiller, as described in chapter 5), Hiller met with the noted rocket scientist, then director of the Marshall Spaceflight Center at Huntsville, Alabama, to discuss the manufacture of satellites. The conversation soon shifted to the huge Saturn V rocket being developed by von Braun and his team at Huntsville, specifically to the scientist's frustration at the prospect of "throwing away" each multimillion dollar moon booster in one-shot use.

Retrieving in midair a spent Saturn V first stage weighing up to 200 tons presented challenges of staggering magnitude, but these were two men who loved technical challenges. "It would require a hell of a big helicopter," Hiller said and they both laughed, but then the businessman told the scientist how it could be done.[14] Von Braun requested a formal proposal from Hiller with which to enlist NASA support.

Hiller engineers worked for three months on the biggest tip-powered flying crane—indeed, the biggest aircraft of any kind—ever formally proposed. So large was it, in fact, that tip engines were the only way to power it; a conventional helicopter of similar size could not be built to fly. This Hiller/NASA recovery vehicle would have featured a multiblade rotor more than 300 feet in diameter. Two or more powerful jet engines on each giant blade would have turned this rotor at 60 rpm, presenting the illusion of slow-motion photography to observers below. Gross weight was estimated at one million pounds.

This flying crane's mission called for loitering up to six hours at 10,000 feet, some 475 miles downrange from Cape Kennedy (the extended endurance to allow for launch delays). Employing some 10,000 pounds of recovery gear, the vehicle would overfly the descending rocket and snag it by its parachutes, after which the cylindrical booster would be winched snugly under the body of the helicopter for return to the Cape. The five-minute recovery window, from the time of sighting until the Saturn first stage had dropped too low, was sufficient to permit the craft's eight-man crew to perform three recovery attempts.

All American Engineering of Wilmington, Delaware, played an essential role in the conceptual development of this proposal. As the innovative manufacturer of arresting gear for carrier aircraft and of aerial recovery systems routinely used to snag spy satellite film canisters high over the Pacific Ocean, All American was uniquely qualified to participate. Company president Charles W. Wendt was so effective in his presentation to NASA that he convinced the space agency of the feasibility of recovering spent rockets in the air.

Expensive as such a helicopter would have been, it was estimated that huge aircraft would have paid for itself with the first several recoveries. Because long-range planning of the nation's space program was beginning to favor the concept of a reusable space shuttle over Saturn-style boosters, however, NASA's booster recovery vehicle was not funded.

The Mature Years

The final decade of the Hiller company's existence—from the mid-1950s through the mid-1960s—saw continuing growth, profitability, and above all creativity. Flying Platforms and the world's first transport-size VTOL aircraft took to the air, and countless other imaginative approaches to flight—many the product of Hiller's new Advanced Research Division (ARD)—were thoroughly investigated. Although the majority of the ARD's fascinating proposals would not be realized for want of military funding, the company's horizons nevertheless broadened until success seemed at last at hand on many fronts.

During this period, Hiller Helicopters would focus its energies on helicopter production, ducted-fan research, and higher-speed VTOL flight. Research-and-development itself would be a major company product; in 1957 alone, for example, the ARD would perform highly classified work for no less than five branches of the Navy, two of the Air Force, and six of Hiller's best customer, the U.S. Army. In fact, so much nonhelicopter work was going on in Palo Alto that on 10 July 1958, the company would formally change its name back to the Hiller Aircraft Corporation.

The conceptual groundwork for virtually all the "new" developments in this period had actually been laid between 1946 and 1951, primarily in the magic year 1947 when the company conducted seminal vertical-takeoff (VTO) studies using powered models. The four-engine XC-142 VTOL transport of the early 1960s dates directly back to that year, as does the wondrous Flying Platform, which is in many ways a modern flying carpet.

At the end of 1947, Hiller took advantage of a trip East to track down aeronautical engineer Charles H. Zimmerman. A longtime NACA engineer, Zimmerman's aggressive pursuit of short-takeoff-and-landing (STOL) capability for aircraft led him to a novel circular-planform approach to aircraft design. The unconventional configuration was promising enough that in 1937 Zimmerman moved to the Chance Vought Aircraft Company in Bridgeport, Connecticut, to direct that company's development of his idea into the experimental V-173 Flying Flapjack and its successor, the Navy's unflown XF5U-1 fighter prototype.

On his own, Charles Zimmerman chose to pursue with equal energy his dream of low-cost flight for humanity. At the close of World War II, this quest led

Invented by aeronautical engineer Charles H. Zimmerman at the close of World War II, the "Flying Shoes" platform was powered by small engines. Evaluated in Palo Alto in 1948, it was flown by shifting one's weight toward the direction chosen, a system termed "kinesthetic control."

him to develop a VTO test rig called the Zimmerman "Flying Shoes." The device consisted of a small platform of light steel tubing with two small two-cycle four-cylinder target drone engines powering upward-facing propellers.

After starting the Flying Shoes, a "pilot" would buckle into its metal bindings and rev up the engines with twist-grip throttles mounted on a long pole connected to the platform by a universal joint (the latter to prevent the pole from tilting the craft like a long lever). Once off the ground, the pilot could fly in any direction merely by shifting his weight—leaning forward to go straight ahead, leaning to the left to go that way, and so on.

Always looking for individuals with new ideas, and intrigued with the Flying Shoes concept, which paralleled ideas of his own, Stanley Hiller gave high priority to visiting Charles Zimmerman at his home in Connecticut. Impressed with the device he saw stored in the engineer's garage, Hiller arranged to have it shipped out to California for evaluation by his company.

The Flying Shoes arrived in Palo Alto early in 1948, where long skids and tether cables were promptly attached for safety. Flown by Frank Peterson, the rig showed promise but was not raised very far off the ground because, lacking an interconnect between the engines, it was difficult to balance the thrust of the power plants. The independently powered propellers also presented the potential for a dangerous accident were one engine to fail.

Zimmerman's Flying Shoes were based on his insight that a neutrally stable platform would result from placing the center

of gravity above the plane of lift; if helicopters with rotors on top are inherently unstable, the reverse is true for flying machines with rotors mounted underneath. That the concept was not intuitively obvious to others became clear to Zimmerman when he first described his work to colleagues. "A number of my friends, all competent engineers," he recalled with some amusement, "laughed at the idea when I mentioned it."[1]

Zimmerman carried his thinking one critical step further: With the plane of lift below the center of gravity, he theorized, a person's instinctual balancing reflexes would suffice to control a vehicle, provided it was small enough. If one could walk or ride a bicycle, one could fly by what the inventor termed "kinesthetic control."

Charles Zimmerman returned to the NACA in 1948 as assistant chief of the Stability Research Division at Wallops Island, Langley, Virginia. There he built a "Jet Board," powered by wind tunnel air-storage spheres, upon which in February 1951 he dramatically proved a person can balance atop a jet of air. (On his first flight, in fact, the inventor failed to realize he was airborne, because controlling the platform by unconscious body motion came naturally.) Zimmerman's follow-on propeller-driven "Whirligig" of 1953—also powered by compressed air—further validated the startlingly simple concept of kinesthetic control.

The success of these efforts in Virginia prompted the Office of Naval Research to suggest that Hiller's company (which had shelved the Flying Shoes in 1948 to get the UH-12-360 into production) might again pursue Zimmerman's concepts, this time mated to the ducted-fan concept of Alexander Satin, chief engineer of the Air Branch in the ONR's Naval Sciences Division. Intrigued with the idea, Hiller agreed, and a contract was signed on 17 September 1953.

An engineering team headed by project engineer Arthur Robertson at Palo Alto set about building upon Zimmerman's pioneering research. Working in isolation on the Model 1031, as the classified project was called, they designed a compact twin-engine platform with coaxial counterrotating propellers encased in a fiberglass ring of airfoil cross-section. In fact, marrying Zimmerman's ideas to Satin's ducted fan produced a machine of surprising efficiency: the propellers produced 60 percent of the lift and the duct produced the remaining 40 percent.

Construction of Hiller Flying Platform Number One began in January 1954 and ended nine months later, with the work proceeding slowly because only fifteen of some nine hundred Hiller employees even knew the classified craft existed. The dark-blue wingless aircraft was five feet in diameter and was light enough to be carried by two men. It was the world's first ducted-fan VTO vehicle to fly successfully, and the first heavier-than-air aircraft capable of being flown from the outset by someone without flight training.

After unmanned evaluation of a fully instrumented duct to determine its airflow characteristics both in and out of ground effect, the three-phase test program moved on to manned testing of the first Flying Platform. Flying Shoes expert Frank Peterson had recently left the company, so Hiller chief test pilot Philip T. Johnston was assigned to the program.

This capable World War II veteran ironically found himself flying a craft requiring absolutely none of the considerable piloting skill he had honed during eighty fighter sweeps over Europe.

Johnston gingerly explored the platform's kinesthetic controllability in a "high-wire" tether arrangement which permitted limited vertical and horizontal flight. The unique vehicle demonstrated unusual but acceptable flight characteristics, so after several weeks the team moved on to the third—and most dramatic—phase of testing.

Hiller's Flying Platform made its first free flight on 27 January 1955. Unfettered, it flew with far greater precision and control authority than its size might have suggested. And it was quick, heeling into tight turns as it zipped smartly through maneuvers. In horizontal flight, however, speed was inherently restricted owing to an uneven distribution of induced flow across the duct (and, to a lesser degree, because of airflow interference by the pilot and the framework on which he stood). The result was that greater lift was developed by the front of the Flying Platform than the rear. When the pilot leaned to tilt the craft in the direction he desired to go, therefore, it "pushed back" enough to retard its speed. Since it still whisked along much faster than a man could run, however, and as this "limitation" added to the vehicle's safety, its developers were well satisfied.

After three months, all secrecy was dropped and the Flying Platform made its debut to surprisingly wide acclaim. A public accustomed to unusual doings at Hiller now had more grist for daydreams; images of privately owned Flying Plat-

*D*eveloped as a classified project for the Office of Naval Research, the Hiller Flying Platform combined Zimmerman's concept of "kinesthetic control" with a ducted fan for high efficiency and a small diameter. The tether cables shown here facilitate early tests and training.

forms once again rekindled dreams of low-cost personal flying machines.

The 29 April 1955 issue of *Collier's* magazine featured Hiller's blue prototype in flight on its cover. "As we watched," the article's authors reported, "Hiller test pilot Phil T. Johnston, hovering several feet in the air, moved a small ring-shaped platform forward and back and from side to side. There was no visible evidence of what was keeping Johnston in the air. Only the staccato bark of engines indicated that here was no form of magic, but a new and revolutionary flying device, forerunner of a possible series of exciting air vehicles unlike anything that has flown before."[2]

The article suggests the particular delight evoked by the imaginative new aircraft: "Because Hiller's flying platform bears such a marked resemblance to the flying saucers that have so captured public fancy, even an expert's first reaction as it rises from the ground is likely to be a mixture of sheer amazement and the urge to chuckle at so comic a concept."[3]

Work was already under way on a second—and safer—unit. The original Flying Platform had each propeller directly driven with no interconnect, a very dangerous situation in the event of an engine failure; such an occurrence at altitude would cause the vehicle to spin out of control, probably with fatal consequences. Succeeding platforms, therefore, would all have a revised drive system linking both propellers through a gearbox so that each engine powered both propellers. Thus deprived of differential throttling for yaw control, these platforms would need underside control vanes to rotate about the vertical axis.

With a life-size weighted dummy at its controls to maintain its center of gravity, the first prototype was mounted in a tiltable frame atop a Hiller pickup truck that raced up and down Moffett Field's long runways. Lacking a wind tunnel, Hiller often availed itself of the Navy base in this manner to obtain low-speed aerodynamic data. The purpose of this particular series of tests was to investigate the transition of ducted fans to horizontal flight, as might be required of VTOL aircraft in the future. Hiller, in fact, was already thinking of futuristic high-performance ducted-fan derivatives.

Two further ducted-fan study contracts were received from the research-oriented ONR. The first was for a rectangular and rather flat giant crane built around four huge ducts with counterrotating fans. The second was for a crane with side-mounted tilting ducts. Neither of these ideas progressed beyond the conceptual stage.

At this juncture, the U.S. Army took over responsibility for funding further developments of the Hiller Flying Platform. But blinded by visions of flying carpets for infantrymen, Army officials failed to appreciate the potential of more exotic ducted-fan vehicles. They wanted simply to enlarge the basic platform for use as a reconnaissance vehicle or for crossing mine fields and other man-made or natural barriers. They also foresaw it as an elevated firing platform for infantry sharpshooters. Accordingly, the Army issued a contract in 1956 for three Hiller YHO-1Bs, or VZ-1s as they were soon rechristened (the new designation denoting research-vehicle status). Later amended to two VZ-1Es (a third was

Secrecy was dropped in April 1955 and the Hiller Flying Platform was unveiled to the public. Phil T. Johnson, Hiller test pilot, demonstrates the craft.

retained by the company), this contract was fulfilled in December 1957 and testing began the following year.

For safety, a third engine was added to permit continued flight even if one engine were to fail. This well-intended safety measure, along with the wider six-foot-diameter duct it necessitated, made these new Flying Platforms so cumbersome that they no longer responded effectively to kinesthetic control. With proportionately less "crew" weight to control it, they were also appreciably less stable. Following unsuccessful efforts to develop aerodynamic control augmentation devices—evaluated by both Hiller and Army pilots—the unwieldy VZ-1Es were soon retired. With the Flying Platform now too big and too unwieldy to be useful to the infantry, the Army lost interest. Hiller's promising kinesthetic-control ducted-fan program came to an abrupt end.

It is worth noting that, eight years after Hiller, another company also began following in the footsteps of Charles Zimmerman (if his Flying Shoes could be said to have footsteps). Beginning in January 1955, Donald de Lackner, president of de Lackner Helicopters of Mount Vernon, New York, flew a platform, with rotors at the bottom, known as the DH-4 Heli-Vector. A more powerful version known as the DH-5 Aerocycle followed soon afterward under ONR sponsorship. Crude in comparison to Hiller's Flying Platforms, these test rigs were similarly controlled by shifting one's weight. Being unducted, however, they were inherently less efficient and needed large-diameter rotors to achieve flight. Unlike the work

undertaken at Palo Alto, the de Lackner program failed to improve significantly upon Zimmerman's own efforts.

Disappointed with the Army's waning interest, the Hiller team sought to salvage whatever support might remain by submitting proposals for logical Flying Platform developments. The first of these was a Flying Jeep with four ducted fans, two at the front and two at the rear. Illustrations of the Hiller Flying Jeep showed an olive-drab vehicle with open seating. It somewhat suggested its ground-based inspiration, although it was a much more substantial vehicle. Powered either by a T58 or two T63 turbine engines, in fact, the craft as proposed by Hiller could lift a standard Army truck. The Hiller Flying Jeep was eminently feasible, as it built directly upon work already accomplished.

Although Hiller alone had the experience to build such a craft, the Army—which was required to solicit competitive bids from industry—awarded aerial jeep contracts to Piasecki; the Aerophysics Development Corporation of Santa Barbara, California (a division of Curtiss-Wright); and Chrysler. None of these manufacturers had much if any experience with ducted fans, and Chrysler had never even built an aircraft! When these contractors failed to produce a viable aerial jeep, the Army canceled the program. For Hiller, it was another frustrating lesson in the arcane workings of procurement.

"We should have spent more of the cost of a proposal on a mock-up," Hiller reflected in later years, observing that a full-size model of the Flying Jeep might

*A*rmy specification of three engines
(for safety, should any one engine fail)
produced Flying Platforms too heavy to
respond well to kinesthetic control.
Courtesy NASM/SI.

well have tipped the scales in its favor.[4] Had there been a "showroom display" model for Army generals to inspect and sit in, American ground forces might well have had Flying Jeeps in their inventory.

A second and more exotic Flying Platform derivative was the proposed Ring-Wing Coleopter, a high-speed aircraft that could take off vertically, fly horizontally using its ducted fan as a circular wing, then land vertically again. Moffett Field tests of Flying Platform Number One, described above, generated data for this project, as did the third VZ-1, which was retained by Hiller as an aerodynamic testbed. High-speed ducted-fan flight research was also sponsored by the Navy, which awarded Hiller a contract to study "ring-wing" horizontal flight.

Phil Johnston actually flew the first-generation Coleopter, evaluating both its aerodynamic controls and its extended duct configuration. Before a true prototype could be built and a full conversion attempted, however, the Army—which sponsored construction of the prototype—canceled the project.

Seven Hiller Flying Platforms in all are believed to have been built. Retired after several years of use, the historic first example in dark-blue ONR paint is now on view at the Hiller Aircraft Museum in Redwood City, California, prior to moving to a projected northern California museum. A second twin-engine Platform in Army colors is on display at the Paul E. Garber Facility in Silver Hill, Maryland, where much of the collection of the Smithsonian Institution's National Air and Space Museum is housed. The VZ-1Es were last reported to be at Princeton University for ducted-fan research at that institution.

The other main thrust of Hiller's vertical-takeoff-and-landing experimentation took a decidedly different and much larger form. Under Air Force sponsorship, a very promising approach to vertical flight proposed by Hiller in 1947 would evolve into the world's first transport-size VTOL aircraft by 1959. Called the X-18, this tilt-wing aircraft powered by two twin-pack engines would, in turn, give rise to a larger four-engine tilt-wing sponsored by three military services and built by three manufacturers. Virtually identical to an earlier internal Hiller proposal, the latter craft would be known as the Vought-Hiller-Ryan XC-142.

Once again, an innovative Hiller project could trace its conceptual roots straight back to the magic year 1947, when Hiller and his team experimented in quarter-scale model form with direct jet lift, ducted fans, tilt-rotors, tilt-wings, and other approaches to vertical flight. The tilt-wing then emerged from these empirical studies as the most promising design approach.[5] The crush of getting the Hiller 360 helicopter into production postponed further efforts in this area, however, as did a lack of military research sponsorship.

When Hiller reactivated its VTOL program in 1953, it generated sufficient Army interest to receive from that service the first contract ever awarded to the aircraft industry for large tilt-wing aircraft research studies. Additional Army funds

*P*roposed in the late 1950s, the Hiller Flying Jeep had a ducted fan at each corner. After soliciting industrywide bids for such a vehicle, the Army issued contracts to manufacturers who, lacking Hiller's ducted-fan expertise, were unable to produce successful vehicles.

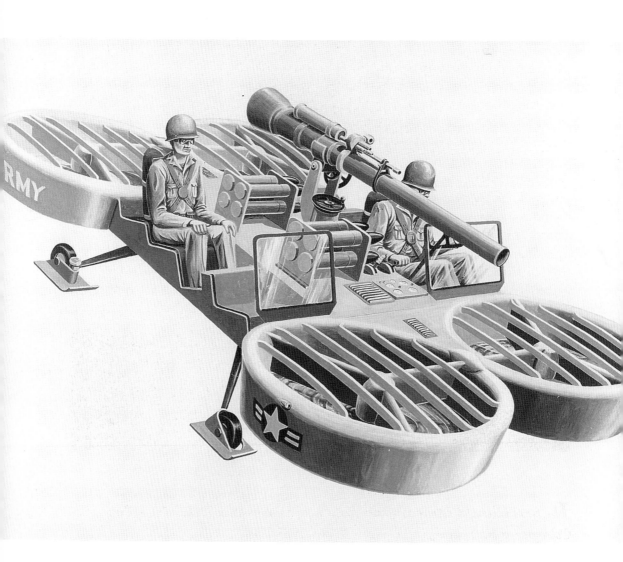

*T*he two Hiller VZ-1Es of *1957* were prototypes of the proposed Hiller Ring-Wing Coleopter, a craft capable of high-speed horizontal flight.

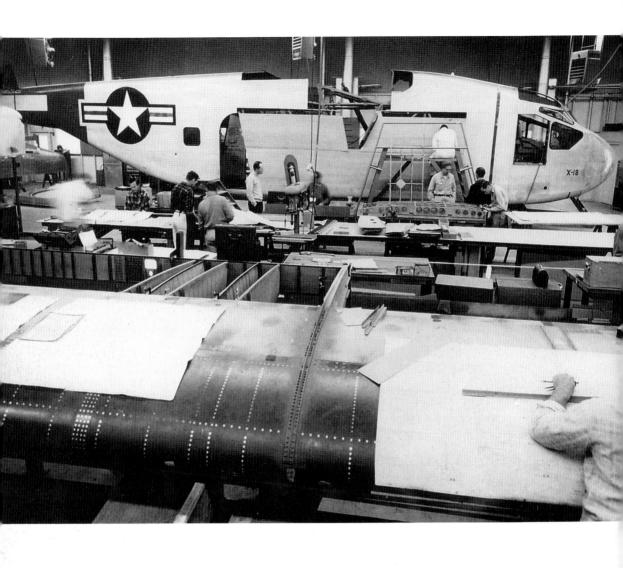

Incorporating the forward and aft fuselage of a Chase YC-122 cargo transport, Hiller's novel X-18 takes shape at Palo Alto. This research plane's steel-tube center fuselage, wings, and internal systems were all new. Courtesy NASM/SI.

The instrument panel and ejection seats are visible in this view from the top of the X-18's fuselage.

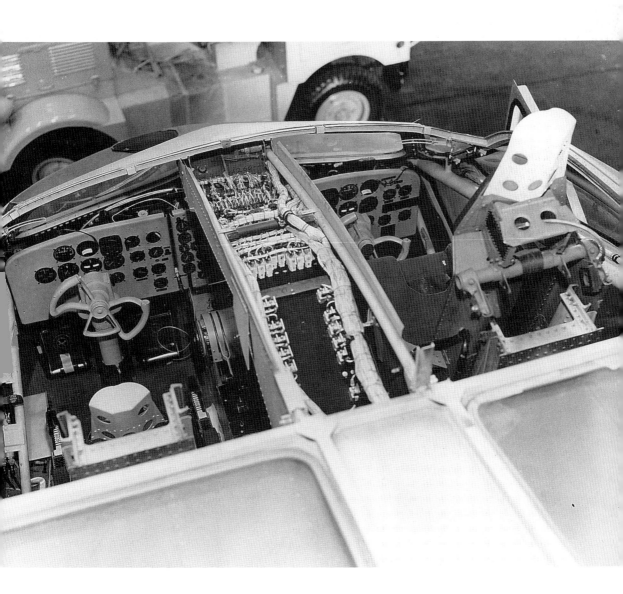

allocated through the Office of Naval Research in 1954 then fostered specific parametric studies of various transport-size tilt-wing aircraft. These were followed by a tilt-wing transport design study contract in 1955.

Frustratingly, the Army could go no further with its pursuit of tilt-wing cargo aircraft because the development of transport planes trespassed on Air Force turf, as delineated by the Key West Accord of 1948. Impressed with Hiller's VTOL work for the Army, however, the Air Force finally decided to support a project of its own. In the winter of 1956, therefore, the USAF awarded Hiller a Phase I contract calling for development of an experimental prototype designated the X-18. Because the greatest need for VTOLs was in the transport role, both for cargo and passengers, the X-18 with its 33,000-pound gross weight would be made large enough to generate useful data on this role which all the services anticipated using.

In the spring of 1956, Hiller's professional staff was reorganized. William Callery, Jr. (nephew of board member Francis Callery) was named assistant chief engineer, administrative; and Wayne Wiesner was named assistant chief engineer, technical (the two men had formerly been director of flight and chief project engineer, respectively). Robert Wagner remained chief engineer.

Department heads of Hiller's Engineering Division under the reorganization included Don Jacoby, chief test-dynamics engineer; Richard Carlson, chief aerostructures engineer; Harold Sigler, chief preliminary design engineer; Robert Anderson, chief project engineer; William Werner, chief administrative engineer; Harvey Holm, experimental manufacturing manager; Harold Westphal, chief draftsman; Joe Stuart, chief special projects engineer; and John Nichols, products planning manager. As ever, hard-working Warren Rockwell continued to run Hiller's Washington, D.C., office.

The Washington facility in fact served as Hiller's main office. For many years he would leave home Sunday evening—by DC-4 propeller airliners in the earlier days—to spend three days in the District of Columbia before returning Wednesday night to spend the rest of the week at Palo Alto. Introduction of the Boeing 707 had made this routine a fraction less onerous by the end of the 1950s.

The Palo Alto company bore Hiller's distinctive stamp even though he was back East half the time. The energetic company president covered every inch of his factory and talked with workers on the shop floor as readily as he did with his vice-presidents. His fingerprints were to be found everywhere, from engineering to marketing, from production to labor relations, and so on. Before going home in the evening, Hiller would usually pass through the engineering offices in order to study work then in progress. Even the best Hiller engineers upon occasion found themselves chided the following morning for failing to think in sufficiently creative terms.

At the annual meeting of Hiller stockholders on 9 March 1956, William A. Blees was elected to the company's board of directors. Retired from a brilliant career in the automotive and aviation industries, Blees was a well-known mar-

With its wing tilted vertically, the X-18 could take off, land, or hover like a helicopter. Courtesy NASM/SI.

keting authority whose expertise would prove valuable to Hiller in his continuing effort to broaden the horizons of his maturing company.

This effort led to the acquisition in March 1958 of California-based Adhesive Engineering Company, one of America's leading producers of aircraft and missile structural bonding materials. Then, on 30 November 1960, after fifteen years of growth without external corporate support, a new era began when Hiller arranged for his company to join the much larger Electric Autolite Company. Heretofore a major supplier to Chrysler, Electric Autolite would soon afterward sell its automotive business to Ford and would restructure under a new name, ELTRA.

The favorable merger preserved Hiller company autonomy while giving it access to a great deal of additional capital. It also substantially increased the value of shares held by Hiller stockholders and, more important from Hiller's perspective, guaranteed them increasing cash dividends. Stanley Hiller, who became a major stockholder and board member of Electric Autolite/ELTRA, had not arranged the merger out of necessity; the Palo Alto company had been profitable right up to the merger. Rather, the president had perceived a need to shift his company to a higher economic plateau for another reason.

Without the economic muscle the merger provided, the time would arrive when Hiller Aircraft would have to choose between scaling back its very serious commitment to research and development, or ending its trend of increasing profitability. Willing to do neither, Hiller found merger to be an excellent third solution which poised the company for an ambitious new level of effectiveness as an aviation manufacturer. Yet another upward step would be taken by the company early in 1964 with the sale by ELTRA of Hiller Aircraft to the Maryland-based Fairchild Stratos Corporation, as described later in this chapter.

As Hiller's first winged aircraft, the X-18 research plane was in fact a convertiplane capable of flight as a conventional aircraft, a helicopter, or a STOL (short-takeoff-and-landing) machine spanning the two. Hiller initiated this program with a canny cost-cutting suggestion that delighted the Air Force. Instead of building a new airplane from scratch, the company elected to "recycle" the nose and tail of a Chase YC-122 transport plane (USAF serial no. 49-2883), to which it would add a new center fuselage, wing, landing gear, and assorted internal systems designed and manufactured in Palo Alto.

Hiller already had his eye on engines for this research plane, these being the two 5,850-shp Allison YT40-A-14 turboprops recently employed, one each, in the experimental Lockheed XFV-1 and Convair XFY-1 tail-sitting "pogo stick" fighter prototypes developed at the instigation of the Navy. Because each T40 "twin pack" unit incorporated two turboshaft power plants coupled together, the X-18 could also be thought of as a four-engine machine despite its twin-engine appearance. A 3,400-pound static-thrust Westinghouse J34-WE-36 turbojet would also be used in the X-18's rear fuselage; this small unit's thrust could be diverted up or down by a deflector to provide pitch control during hover and forward flight at speeds too low for the elevators to be effective.

Project engineer for the X-18 was Percy R. ("Bunny") Dowden, whose previous efforts included the ten-turboprop-engine Saunders Rowe Princess airliner in England, one of the largest flying boats ever built. Otto Santoff was head of production. The aircraft was built in a separate facility along one edge of the Hiller property line. Here, an entirely new one-piece wing, forty-eight feet long, was designed and built, along with a metal-clad steel-tube fuselage center section through which the wing would pivot a full ninety degrees. Final assembly was completed at Moffett Field, where the unique craft (USAF serial no. 57-3078) was officially rolled out on 8 December 1958.

Here at last was a transport plane capable of taking off normally with the wing horizontal, with a very short ground run with the wing inclined (STOL), or straight up with the wing vertical (VTOL). Capable of flying faster than a conventional transport plane its size, the X-18 could also stop still in the air or cruise slowly for search-and-rescue duties. Throughout its flight envelope, it would remain more or less level.

Denied normal landing facilities or smooth terrain, proposed military developments of the X-18 could land in as little space as a large helicopter. Civil airliner versions could exploit this capability, thus bypassing crowded airports and providing direct service to urban centers, perhaps obviating the need for constructing costly new airports in the future.

An eight-foot wind-tunnel model of the X-18 was thoroughly tested in the National Aeronautics and Space Administration's low-speed wind tunnel at Langley, Virginia. NASA (the new name of the revised National Advisory Committee for Aeronautics under the Space Act of 1958) thoroughly evaluated all aspects of the Hiller prototype, including the transition from vertical to horizontal flight and back.

Following ground-testing, including speed runs at different wing angles, the X-18 was moved from the Moffett Naval Air Station—home also to NASA's Ames Research Center—to Edwards Air Force Base in the California desert. A Hiller crew of fourteen engineers and technicians accompanied the plane for the duration of its testing. On 20 November 1959, Hiller test pilots George Bright and Bruce Jones took the X-18 off the dry lake bed airplane-style at 105 knots for a first flight that turned out to be an unexpectedly short hop to fourteen feet of altitude.

"It jumped off the runway unbelievably fast," Bright reported, but the crew's exhilaration evaporated an instant later when part of the overhead canopy blew off with a bang.[6] Engineering data and previous testing had not disclosed just how great the suction would be over the roof with such huge propellers set so close to the fuselage; as it was, the X-18's brute power had literally sucked the top windows out. A somewhat rattled crew turned back to the field for an uneventful downwind landing.

The next flight four days later lasted fourteen minutes and included a climb to 4,000 feet and acceleration to 170 knots. With this success, the test program quickly settled into routine. The X-18 proved to be surprisingly docile for a craft with a thrust-to-weight ratio so great that takeoff acceleration to over 100 mph generally took less than five seconds. Rate of climb was 6,000 feet per minute while top speed was limited to just 250 mph for structural reasons. Empty weight was 26,500 pounds and gross weight was 33,000 pounds.

On the twentieth flight during cruise with a 20–30 degree angle of wing incidence, the pitch control of one propeller suddenly malfunctioned. The prototype rolled uncontrollably and entered a spin. Electing not to eject, pilots Bright and Jones instead managed a recovery at dangerously low altitude and landed safely at Edwards without further incident.

Having accomplished 80 percent of its stated goals at a total cost of $6 million, the program now came to a premature halt and the X-18 was grounded.[7] One reason for this was an expected instability in the pitch-and-roll axes during hovering flight. During hover, with the wing in the vertical position, pitch control depended upon deflected jet thrust at the rear, roll control upon differential throttling of the engines, and yaw control upon differential action of the ailerons bathed in the airflow of the huge propellers. Earlier tests had already disclosed that the Allisons—which, being turbine engines, needed time to spool up or down—responded too slowly to throt-

tling to ensure crisp roll-control during hover. The specter of engine or propeller problems having been raised by the X-18's near loss, a prudent end to the already largely successful program was felt to be in order.

The single disappointment for the Hiller team was that the halt had been called before the X-18 had made a full conversion in the air between horizontal and vertical flight.[8] Flight tests had revealed the need for extensive wing modifications before a full conversion could be performed; without such modification, the prototype encountered extreme buffet.

Another reason for terminating the test program was the Air Force's desire to put the X-18 through ground-effect simulation tests on a special teststand then being built by Gilmore Industries. Tests begun in June 1963 ended inconclusively shortly afterward when the stand, designed to support 75,000 pounds, failed while carrying the far lighter X-18. Sadly, its usefulness now past, this historic Hiller VTOL research plane was disassembled and scrapped.

In the fall of 1958, meanwhile, Hiller Aircraft had begun work on a successor to the X-18 which evolved into the unbuilt Model 1085B. In meetings with the government's Perkins Committee, which had been convened at the Forrestal Research Center in Princeton, New Jersey, engineers John B. Nichols and Joe Stuart surveyed the wide range of VTOL and V/STOL options for a next-generation military transport.[9] Their summary of Hiller company findings on the relative merits of the various approaches to vertical flight led the committee to recommend that a four-engine

The world's first transport-size VTOL aircraft flies with T-28 escort high over the California desert.

tilt-wing transport like the 1085B be developed for the military services.

In 1960, the Department of Defense unveiled its U.S. Tri-Service Assault Transport Program. Announcement of this industrywide request for proposals (RFP) for a multiservice V/STOL transport caused other and larger aircraft companies suddenly to show keen interest in convertible aircraft. Although the Perkins Committee had recommended in favor of Hiller's tilt-wing approach, the Department of Defense RFP left the specific method for achieving vertical flight up to the manufacturer.

While contracts are ostensibly awarded solely on the merits of each company's proposal, in fact such decisions are sometimes "spread around" with an eye to maintaining the financial health of manufacturers and the diversity of the nation's production base. Such awards are also, of course, influenced by those politicians whose constituencies stand to gain or lose with the final outcome.

By now savvy to the politics of military procurement, Stanley Hiller had dispatched his vice-president of engineering and research, Sydney Sherby, to Washington, D.C., to find out which aerospace company was due to win the next major contract. Sherby, a retired Navy captain, learned the list was topped by Vought, the large Texas-based manufacturer of fixed-wing aircraft. Hiller accordingly approached Vought to join forces, and the Texas giant agreed. Ryan in southern California was also enlisted for this Tri-Service Transport team.

Being a near neighbor of giant Convair in San Diego, the small Ryan Aircraft Company lay in a part of the country which traditionally enjoyed strong pro-aviation congressional representation. The company (famous as the builder of Charles Lindbergh's *Spirit of St. Louis* in 1927) had flown a number of small VTOL research aircraft of its own, a fact which further helped chances. Lastly, Ryan brought the number of aircraft builders to three, matching the number of military services sponsoring the VTOL transport. The appealing symmetry of three services plus three manufacturers was thought to have positive "PR" value.

Already a national authority on aircraft technology in his early forties, a Naval Academy graduate, and a rated pilot with a master's in aeronautical engineering, Sydney Sherby had retired as a captain from the Office of Naval Research (he had headed its Air Branch and Naval Sciences Division) to join Hiller at the end of 1958. In Palo Alto, he had assumed responsibility for both the Engineering Division headed by chief engineer Robert A. Wagner and the Advanced Research Division under Frank Heileman. With Bob Anderson and others from Palo Alto, Sherby now traveled many times to Texas to initiate the cooperative tilt-wing program with Vought.

Hiller's Model 1085B proposal initially met with resistance from Vought engineers, who strongly favored a different VTOL approach. Carefully prepared presentations by key Hiller engineers, supported by reams of data, finally persuaded the larger company that a tilt-wing was indeed the way to proceed and a crisis was averted. Convinced at last, Vought adopted the Hiller aircraft as the basis of design for its effort.

Ten industry teams submitted propos-

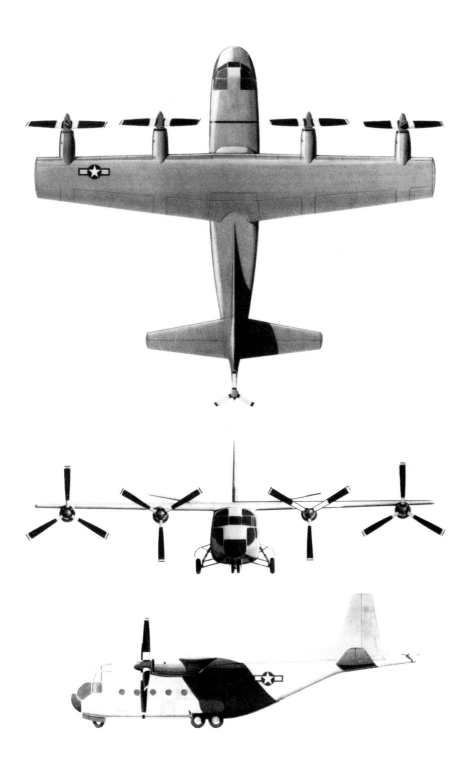

*H*iller's proposed Model 1085B, a follow-on to the X-18, formed the design basis
for the Vought-Hiller-Ryan XC-142A which so closely resembles it.

als to the Navy, which administered the competition, in April 1961. Their submissions included tilt-wings, tilt-rotors, tilt-ducts, and fan-in-wing and lift-jet concepts. Hiller's strategy proved to be faultless as the Vought-Hiller-Ryan VHR-447 was proclaimed the winner. Procured under the designation XC-142A, the resulting aircraft was virtually indistinguishable from the Hiller 1085B except for being stubbier all around, the better to fit aboard the Navy's ships.

Vought, senior partner in the effort, would build all of the XC-142A's airframe, except the aft fuselage and engine nacelles which would be built by Ryan. As these companies lacked the necessary experience, Hiller would design and build the lightweight mechanical shafting-and-gearbox propeller interconnect needed to preserve hovering stability in the event any of the craft's engines failed. The Palo Alto company would also construct the aircraft's ailerons, flaps, and various subsystems.

Five experimental XC-142As were built initially for evaluation. Each had four 2,805 shp General Electric T64 turboprops driving fifteen-and-a-half-foot-diameter propellers plus an upward-facing propeller at the rear. With a wingspan of 67.5 feet and a gross weight of just under 40,000 pounds, the XC-142As were the largest VTOL aircraft ever built. Able to fly from 0 to 430 mph, this unique transport made its first flight on 29 September 1964, its first hovering flight on 29 December, and its first full transition between vertical and horizontal flight on 11 January 1965.

By this time, the Navy had backed out of the XC-142A program, which was turned over to the Air Force. Although reasonably successful overall, this tilt-wing test program experienced accidents and technical difficulties stemming from the newness of VTOL transport operations in general, and the high percentage of unproven components this emerging technology demanded. In the end, however, America's growing military involvement in Vietnam killed any hopes for volume production. Because of a redirection of funds toward the war effort, no additional C-142s were produced.

The X-18 had been built in a separate building to the west of the main factory at Palo Alto. A thousand feet in the other direction, to the east across the main parking lot, Hiller's innovative Advanced Research Division quietly performed fascinating—and generally highly classified—work on a variety of government and company projects. First announced in June 1955 just after ground was broken, this high-security division—the vertical flight industry's first "skunk works" in the Lockheed tradition—officially opened on November first. A smaller version of the main plant's engineering department, this separate facility devoted to innovation had offices for scientists and engineers, a laboratory and a shop, a drafting room, administrative and secretarial help, and a reception area constantly manned by security-conscious personnel.

An interesting observation by Stanley Hiller had given rise to the Advanced Research Division. "We found that we

*W*inner of a contract for a tri-service VTOL transport plane, the Vought-Hiller-Ryan XC-142A of 1964 demonstrates its ability to fly like a helicopter. With a gross weight of over 40,000 pounds and a top speed of 430 mph, the XC-142A remains the largest VTOL airplane ever to fly. Five were built.

couldn't mix our very talented engineers with our regular engineering department," he later explained, "so we gave them a separate building, separate funding, separate management. The extremely talented people there came up with the weirdest wonders."[10]

Administrative head of the ARD was retired Major General Frank A. Heileman, the mechanical engineer and veteran of World War I who had already proved so valuable as a company director. Beneath him were such brilliant minds as Gerhard J. Sissingh, in charge of "aerophysics"; Elbert R. Sargent, chief of propulsion; and F. David Schnebly, head of operations research. Responsible for realizing the ideas of these individuals and their staffs in three-dimensional test devices was longtime Hiller employee Edward Bennett, now in charge of the ARD's fully equipped shop. The prototypes and experimental rigs built day-to-day by Bennett and his group were often tested outdoors in the ARD's courtyard, which by careful design was screened from possible observation.

Away from the daily obligations, frustrations, distractions, and interruptions of life in the hectic main plant, ARD personnel could freely explore all manner of intriguing pursuits, the most unusual of which may have been antigravitational studies, which remain classified at the time of this writing. "We had some major projects running through there," Hiller recalls, "perhaps not major in dollars but certainly in what they might lead to in the future."[11]

One means of achieving VTO flight studied by Dr. Sissingh, for example, was circulation control via a "jet-flap rotor."

The basis of this rotor was the discovery in Germany in 1938 that a sheet of air ejected from the trailing edge of an airfoil at a downward angle induced substantial additional lift. Investigation of this phenomenon—rediscovered in England in 1952 as the "jet flap"—also revealed that the added thrust given the wing when the jet flap was in operation actually exceeded the horizontal thrust component of its jet stream at the wing trailing edge.

A Göttingen-trained specialist in stabilization and rotary wing design, Dr. Sissingh had previously worked for helicopter pioneer Anton Flettner and the *Aerodynamische Versuchsanstalt* (Aerodynamic Research Institute) in Germany and the British Government at Farnborough. He had also worked at Kellett Aircraft in America. His close professional contacts around the world—in part responsible for Hiller performing the first jet-flap research in the United States—were invaluable to the success of the ARD.

Sissingh proposed to adapt the jet-flap principle to rotor blades. Such a system would yield greater helicopter speeds and replacement of the traditional mechanical cyclic control with cyclic variation of the air-mass flow or jet-deflection angle. Impressed with his calculations, the Office of Naval Research awarded Hiller a contract to fund a full investigation of these intriguing possibilities.

This attempt to develop a practical jet-flap rotor in the latter 1950s was frustrated by inadequate engine power. The limitation having subsequently been eliminated by the advent of small but very powerful helicopter turbine packs, the

Rough, improvised airfields were no problem for the XC-142, which could tilt its wing for remarkably short takeoffs even with a heavy load. Although STOL takeoffs saved fuel, the transport—load permitting—needed no runway at all.

possibility of a working jet-flap rotor has again been investigated in recent years (the Sikorsky X-Rotor).

Elbert Sargent's Propulsion Division, meanwhile, carried to new heights Hiller's pioneering work with power plants. Full-size working "hardware" of the novel engines his group proposed were built and tested, and the results of these tests laid the groundwork for a variety of unique flying machines. Some unconventional ARD power plants even made possible the redesign of traditionally non-flying objects into aerial vehicles. To the Army, for example, Hiller would propose a bridge capable of flying where needed by bottlenecked troops; to the Navy, as described below, Hiller would propose a submarine able to travel above the waves as well as below. Seemingly the stuff of science fiction, these proposals were made in all seriousness by many of the best engineers in the field.

Sargent's group began with an intriguing observation: From the forty to fifty pulse-jet and follow-on engines Hiller had so far built and tested, the fact emerged that the intermittent flow of pulsed combustion offers a better transfer of energy than steady flow. The Propulsion Division, therefore, dedicated itself to maximizing the energy transfer taking place with each pulse. Today's fuel-efficient pulse furnaces to heat buildings are one outgrowth of this avenue of research.

Ray Lockwood was a key player in this effort. At that time, the young Hiller engineer probably understood more about unsteady flow than anybody else in the United States. Lockwood would in fact contribute heavily to development of

a number of "augmented flow" engines, this term describing power plants in which energy transfer has been boosted in some manner.

Under Navy sponsorship, Hiller ARD intermittent-flow research produced a special burner called the "resonant combustor." Based on earlier sonic-engine development, the resonant combustor used the energy of sound propagation alone to increase pressure in a valveless or open combustion chamber. The challenge facing Sargent's group was to devise a chamber configuration and fuel-injection arrangement to maximize fuel-air compression before pulsed combustion; the efficiency of their resonant combustor attests to their success in this quest.

Next came the Hiller "pulse reactor," an unusual engine with a phenomenal kick. This low-weight high-thrust augmented intermittent-flow engine could literally be bent, wrapped around obstacles, or tied into knots and still function (much the way a straight horn can be bent into a bugle and still sound the same). Pulse reactors were an airframe designer's dream; unlike conventional power plants, they could be squeezed into wings, wheel wells, and other tight spaces. Sponsored primarily by the Navy, pulse-reactor development also received supplementary Army funds.

Hiller took collapsible, horseshoe-shaped pulse reactors and lined them up diagonally in streamlined boxes with clamshell doors on top. When power was needed for vertical flight, the doors would pop open, allowing the engines to swing to the vertical, extend to operating length, and start. The more power one needed, the longer the box, the minimal frontal area of which remained constant for efficient horizontal flight. Hiller called this concept the "lift package." Affix enough lift packages to lightweight spans, and the idea of flying bridges suddenly begins to sound reasonable.

Along with intermittent-flow engines such as the pulse reactor, the ARD simultaneously pursued development of continuous-flow and continuous-flow-to-intermittent-flow units. The best of the former was the "annular ejector," an interesting power plant from which combustion efflux was not immediately expelled. Instead, the exhaust was repeatedly mixed with additional augmented air to reap multiple transfers of energy. Costs of developing the annular ejector were shared by the Hiller company and the Army, which acted through the Office of Naval Research.

Groundwork for the ejector was laid by "entrainment-of-air" experiments conducted by the ARD. The term refers to getting an airflow to do what one wants by creatively taking advantage of known physical phenomena such as the Coanda effect. An extreme use of entrainment proposed by Sargent and Lockwood was based on laboratory tests demonstrating that a rotating column of air could actually be bent into a "U" shape.

The two engineers enlisted just such a horseshoe of air to turn a normal airplane into a VTOL aircraft by proposing that a "vortex generator" be built into each wing. Driven by engine power, these generators (not to be confused with static aerodynamic tabs of the same name, commonly found on the wings of jet aircraft) would create a tornadolike vortex arcing from the top of one wing to the other,

thereby greatly lowering the ambient air pressure. Since the difference in air pressure above versus below the wings defines lift, the vortex would create lift at zero airspeed to "suck" the aircraft off the ground. In forward flight, the generators would be covered and the aircraft would fly conventionally.

The ARD's vortex-lift study confirmed that a rotating column of air could indeed be produced on a scale large enough to bridge the wings of a military airplane. Such imaginative thinking hints at an underlying implicit assumption, far more prevalent in the 1950s than today, that significant new aerodynamic properties remain to be discovered and harnessed.

Another ARD attempt to give an existing aircraft VTOL versatility involved the use of collapsible annular ejectors in the wings of a Convair B-58 Hustler. A "hot" machine, which then played an important role in America's strategic arsenal, the supersonic USAF bomber needed very long prepared runways to operate. The prospect of giving it short field or even vertical flight capability, therefore, commanded substantial military interest, and a contract was issued. That the full-scale engine hardware built and tested by Hiller was never installed in a B-58 might have had something to do with the fact that the Navy, and not the Air Force, funded the program.

Then there was the ARD's fascinating AR-13 Ductoplane of 1958. In this proposed Army high-speed observation aircraft, the futuristic fuselage incorporated a ducted fan set between its bubble-canopied cockpit and a delta wing with its center section articulated to deflect thrust for hovering. Powered by two Lycoming T55 turboprop engines driving counterrotating propellers within the duct, the AR-13—a lineal descendent of the Flying Platform—had an estimated top speed of 400 knots.

Knowing that pulse reactors could make almost anything fly, Hiller proposed a flying submarine to the Navy in 1964. With rows of pulse reactors tucked into its hull providing sufficient aggregate thrust, a moderate-size submersible under attack could burst from the waves and fly swiftly—albeit not far—to safer waters.

Being too creative has its drawbacks, of course. Known throughout its history for unconventional and imaginative thinking, Hiller Aircraft perennially ran the danger of easy dismissal by procurement officers. The flying submarine undoubtedly crossed this line once again, although the project as proposed appeared technically feasible. The fact that full-size pulse reactors—each packing a remarkable wallop—had by now been thoroughly tested failed to convince incredulous military procurement officials (perhaps because of the noise produced by pulse reactors). With the shelving of the flying-submarine concept, Hiller's longtime testing of lift packages came to an end.

In the latter 1950s, Hiller Aircraft became the first American company to purchase and employ a water tunnel. Obtained from Europe, the device—a low-cost alternative to wind tunnels—yielded valuable high-speed helicopter flight data. It was based on an expedient practiced by Focke-Wulf and other German companies during World War II which offset the lack of wind tunnels by towing models and full-size aircraft

structures under the surface of lakes. The tunnel literally used the dense medium of water at low velocity to simulate high-velocity airflow. Simple Reynolds number computations translated the hydrodynamic results into useful aerodynamic data.

Water tunnel research contributed to an ARD proposal dated 24 January 1958, for a wingless, high-performance missile resupply aircraft. Considered by Elbert Sargent to have been the most promising of all the ARD's unbuilt projects, this radical craft drew its inspiration from Lieutenant General James M. Gavin, a formidable champion of Army aviation whose influential views often ran afoul of Key West restrictions.[12]

In the 1950s, U.S. military theorists ascribed too much significance to missiles. One of the lessons of the Vietnam War a decade later was that tactical missiles complement other weapon systems but do not supersede them. In the meantime, however, the Army planned for a new kind of ground warfare in which tactical missiles replaced cumbersome field artillery.

At an Army conference held at Fort Bliss, Texas, in the spring of 1957, General Gavin observed that the battlefield value of quickly expended tactical missiles depends on rapid resupply, a capability the Army did not have. To address this lack, Elbert Sargent and his team came up with the Hiller AR-7, a resupply vehicle capable of delivering Dart, Little John, Hawk, Nike Ajax, and other tactical missiles to Army ground forces in the heat of battle. Looking like an oversize X-tailed jet fighter except for the striking absence of wings, the AR-7 was in fact a radically new approach to VTOL flight. Sargent's bold proposal carried to its ultimate conclusion the concepts of Burnelli, Bellanca, Lippisch, Northrop, and other designers of flying-wing and lifting-body aircraft.

However new on the aviation scene, the AR-7 could trace its development straight back to 1947 when the then-small Hiller company undertook pioneering evaluations of vertical flight alternatives. In addition to tilt-wings and tilt-rotors, Hiller and his team had evaluated "jet lift" or "direct lift" using large quarter-scale models raised by pulse jets.

If the aircraft proposed by ARD personnel had enough thrust to hover, it would also have enough power to fly at very high speed. The fuselage itself would serve as an airfoil, and transition to forward flight—difficult in many approaches to VTOL—would be simple because of the nature of jet lift.

Powered by six J85 turbojets, the AR-7 had an anticipated top speed of .9 Mach, or 595 knots (684 mph) on the deck. If there were any reason to gain altitude, the missile resupply aircraft could climb at an estimated 51,000 feet per minute. Turning without wings was, of course, another matter entirely; its cornering radius at sea level was a full three miles. Getting the AR-7 to the battlefield would be no problem; the wingless craft fit without disassembly into the cargo bay of a Lockheed C-130, the standard military transport plane.

Hiller engineers cited low operating costs and the fact that the AR-7 was not "breakthrough dependent"; in other words, it could be built right away with off-the-shelf technology. The fact that

this unusual craft was wingless now had special significance. A *de facto* shift in the restrictions on Army aviation was in progress, bringing concessions on helicopter gross weights at the expense of conventional aircraft. Eventually, it seemed, the Army would have helicopters of all sizes, but no fixed-wing airplanes.

By default, the AR-7 fell into the latter category even though it had no wings, fixed or otherwise. Wingless or not, this high-performance aircraft invaded prime Air Force turf and ran afoul of Key West restrictions. For this reason, and perhaps because the VTO aircraft was too radical for its time, the interesting project was not funded.

Flying Platforms, tilt-wings, wingless aircraft, and other wide departures from standard helicopter development were all part of a calculated effort by Hiller to free his company from the limited profits remaining to be made in the fiercely competitive light helicopter field. As yet unrealized opportunities awaited the first company to implement new avenues of vertical flight. In the meantime, however, helicopters remained very much the primary business at Palo Alto.

Work had begun late in 1954 on a new helicopter in response to a Navy contract calling for development of a one-man escape-and-rescue vehicle for use by the U.S. Marine Corps. Of some thirty responses to an industrywide request for proposals the preceding year, Hiller in California and Gyrodyne in New York produced winning submittals and were awarded development contracts.

*T*he Rotorcycle climbed at 825 feet per minute and cruised for 45 minutes at over 50 miles per hour. Disassembled, it fit into a tube two feet in diameter which could be dropped to downed pilots.

Hiller's entry, the XROE-1 Rotorcycle, made its first flight in November 1956. Looking more like an insect than a helicopter, and weighing just 290 pounds, the Rotorcycle was developed specifically for rescue, escape and evasion, and "small unit tactical missions."[13] The XROE-1—the work of chief engineer Robert Wagner's Engineering Division rather than the Advanced Research Division—climbed at 825 feet per minute and cruised for 45 minutes at over 50 miles per hour. Power was supplied by a four-cylinder two-cycle Nelson engine rated at 45 hp. The primary evaluator of this minimal flying machine was Richard L. Peck, then Hiller Aircraft's chief test pilot.

During the Korean War, a fighter pilot downed behind enemy lines in rugged country had no helicopters available to pick him up before his position was overrun by enemy forces. A Hiller Rotorcycle, packed in collapsed form into a streamlined container only two feet in diameter, could be parachuted to the downed flier who, without tools, could assemble it in five minutes and fly off to safety. Fighter aircraft would provide top cover to the Rotorcycle if necessary; fighters could also deliver them to downed pilots as Rotorcycle containers were designed to be carried on underwing bomb racks or even in place of wingtip fuel tanks.

Fantastic as it sounds, the precision-engineered Rotorcycle could indeed be readied for flight in just minutes since assembly required only the insertion of a few quick-release pins. As for flying, the XROE proved remarkably stable despite its size because it featured Hiller's Rotormatic cyclic. The servo-rotor paddles were rigged to accommodate the exaggerated control inputs of inexperienced pilots, although a quick readjustment on the ground was all that was needed to provide seasoned pilots with crisper control response.

Having also won a Rotorcycle contract, the Gyrodyne Company of Long Island, New York, took a different approach to meet the Navy's requirements. The XRON-1, which flew a full year before Hiller's XROE-1, incorporated twin coaxial rotors and a wheeled landing gear. Despite its larger size, Gyrodyne's machine was substantially less stable than the Hiller entry, and the company also failed to meet the military's requirement for collapsibility.

The Navy procured five YROE-1s (the "Y" prefix denoting pre-production status) for evaluation beginning late 1958, and the Hiller company built additional Rotorcycles of its own to use as demonstrators for potential foreign sales (Dick Peck actually flew an ROE-1 through the Alps on a European promotional tour, which led to limited Rotorcycle production under license in West Germany). Despite the success of the machine in testing by the U.S. Marines, however, the Rotorcycle had too low a procurement priority to generate volume-production contracts. The few examples of this trim little machine which today survive are a fascinating tribute to the ability of their manufacturer to rise to challenges of all sizes.

The Smithsonian Institution's National Air and Space Museum in Washington, D.C., still occasionally receives letters and telephone calls from enthusiasts hoping to find both Hiller Rotorcycles and

*T*he Los Angeles Police Department
used this 12-C, LAPD's first helicopter,
for traffic patrol beginning in April
1956. Courtesy A. W. B. Vincent.

Hiller Flying Platforms. That both types continue to capture the public imagination after so many years is hardly surprising; small and simple enough to be privately maintained and flown at minimal expense, each would be the unquestioned hit of any air show. While the NASM collection preserves an example of both types, its curators cannot help would-be restorers with their search.

Against the busy backdrop of Hornets, Rotorcycles, VTOL experiments, and ARD projects, Hiller consistently devoted top priority to improving successive versions of the UH-12 series. The quality of the production aircraft rolling off the Palo Alto assembly lines already bore proof that Hiller's facilities and engineering abilities were second to none, yet the best was still to come.

Army H-23Bs already in service were supplemented beginning in late 1955 by the first Hiller H-23Cs, a substantially revised version featuring a rounder canopy for more room and better visibility, especially downward where the metal fuselage lip had been replaced with more Plexiglas. Other changes included a redesigned instrument panel a third smaller than that of previous models, and a new carburetor that reduced pilot workload by automatically adjusting the fuel-air mixture according to altitude. Canada received H-23Cs in 1956, the same year Hiller brought a commercial version called the 12-C to market.

On 3 April 1956, the new Hiller H-23D flew for the first time. Largely unheralded in the annals of rotary-wing flight, this significant event marks the emergence of a new plateau of piston-powered helicopter technology. Constant refinement of the UH-12 series, bolstered by a massive company commitment to produce the finest possible helicopter, brought about a true quantum leap in helicopter technology.

More than just a refinement of earlier models (each of which had stood at the forefront of the fast-advancing state of the art when built), the revised UH-12D embodied virtually every "wish-list" improvement its design team could come up with over years of effort, testing, and operational analysis. Backed by a management willing to shoulder high development costs in order to "do it right," and further subsidized by Army funding, the new helicopter boasted several major innovations in addition to countless lesser refinements. The first of the late-generation Hillers, the UH-12D would bring reciprocating-engine helicopter technology to a zenith unsurpassed to this day.

To begin with, the new H-23D was designed to fly 1,000 hours between transmission and drive-train overhauls. All helicopters then in existence required frequent major overhaul of these areas, which greatly increased their operating costs. The earlier Hiller H-23C, by way of comparison, could operate only some 300 hours between dynamic-system overhauls.

When a Hiller study showed that it should be possible to design gears, bearings, and lubrication systems in such a way as to reach this 1,000-hour mark, the Army immediately offered developmental support; as the largest operator of heli-

A duel between James Bond, played by Sean Connery, and a Hiller 12-C thrilled movie audiences in From Russia with Love *(United Artists, 1964).* Courtesy New York Public Library for the Performing Arts; Astor, Lenox and Tilden Foundations; Billy Rose Theatre Collection.

copters in the United States, it perceived huge potential savings in the program which, if successful, would put pressure upon the rest of the industry to follow suit.[14] At the same time the Army ordered its first H-23C (serial no. 55-4060), therefore, it also ordered two H-23D prototypes (serial nos. 55-4061 and 55-4062). The success of these evaluation aircraft in meeting the manufacturer's claims led to three orders in 1957 and 1958 totaling almost $16 million for 316 aircraft at an average cost of $50,000 per aircraft plus spare parts.

The Hiller H-23D incorporated all that had been learned over seven years from some 900 helicopters already produced at Palo Alto. Obvious external differences between the D and preceding models were all-metal rotor blades; a lightweight skid landing gear; and the relocation of its tail rotor to the left side, with a concomitant relocation to the right of the horizontal stabilizer, to eliminate a harmonic vibration in earlier Hillers known as "tail-boom buzz." Tail vibration was further reduced by using zero-offset flapping hinges on the tail rotor blades.

Lesser changes included a solenoid starter, an automatic throttle-collective interconnect to maintain constant rotor RPMs during collective pitch changes, accurate electric fuel gauges, better cabin heating, lightweight main-rotor scissors to reduce cyclic feedback, the elimination of collective stick forces, a 50-ampere generator (twice the capacity of H-23Cs) now driven from the transmission for greater accessibility, the use of laminated-metal tension-torsion bars in the tail rotor (paralleling the use of T-T bars in

the main rotor), and a larger 46-gallon fuel cell in the fuselage pan.

Power was supplied by a new 250-hp Lycoming VO-435 engine topped by a new unlimited-life transmission, which, despite its smaller size, could accept 40 percent more power than the unit it replaced. A revised engine mount permitted the engine to be removed independently of the transmission and rotor. Gross weight was increased by 200 pounds to 2,700 pounds, while top speed was raised to 95 mph (76 mph with two external litters attached).

The first production H-23Ds reached the Army in December 1957. Most went directly to the Army's Primary Helicopter School, which had relocated in July 1956 to Camp Wolters in Mineral Wells, Texas, from San Marcos, Texas. This spacious facility, operated in part by civil contractors, was a large heliport with marked runways and lights for night flying, a control tower, maintenance facilities, and classrooms. Not far away were four "stage" fields—80-acre satellite bases with landing strips and taxiways. In between were plenty of trees and rough terrain for honing landing and takeoff skills. Beginning with 120 H-23Ds, Camp Wolters continued to grow as helicopters became ever more central to Army aviation. Altogether some 600 Hiller H-23s would eventually accumulate in excess of three million flight hours at this training base. Camp Wolters's Hiller Ravens—as the Army christened the H-23 in 1957—represented the largest concentration of helicopters anywhere in the world.

By 1958, reinvestment in state-of-the-art machine tools and other equipment per-

*F*irst flown in 1956 and delivered to the Army late the following year, the Hiller
H-23D boasted the industry's first 1,000-hour transmission and drive train.
Compared with earlier Hillers and other helicopters requiring overhaul after
a few hundred flight hours, the H-23D offered increased reliability and
reduced maintenance costs.

mitted production of fully 80 percent of the H-23D helicopter right at Palo Alto. Even the optically perfect windshield was now made in-house. This marked increase in on-site fabrication resulted in a higher profit margin than had been possible with the heavily subcontracted early models.

Although granted a production certificate on 23 December 1957, the Model 12D (a civil counterpart to the H-23D) was not marketed; instead, Hiller kept the commercial 12-C in production until ready to unveil an even better version known in prototype form as the H-23D-1. The now-classic Hiller Model 12E was introduced on 23 September 1958 and certified on 6 January 1959. It would remain in production well into the 1980s.

"Stan Hiller's 12E is the best lightweight three-place helicopter ever built," asserts Delford M. Smith, whose Oregon helicopter operation has evolved over the years into Evergreen International Aviation, one of the world's largest all-service aviation companies.[15] Smith logged thousands of hours in 12Es in agricultural, forestry, and construction duties, flying out to oil rigs, and even saving lives on occasion. "Frequently when a person's life was hanging in the balance," states Smith, himself a winner of the helicopter industry's Fred Feinberg award for a heroic rescue, "the 12E was an angel of mercy."[16]

To the original 360's stability and maneuverability, the 12-B's ruggedness, and the 12D's reduced maintenance, the E model now added the final ingredient necessary for lasting commercial success: remarkable performance for a piston-powered helicopter. With a 305-hp Lycoming VO-540 engine, the Model 12E could routinely haul underslung loads weighing a full thousand pounds. Top speed was 96 mph, cruise speed was 90 mph, and gross weight was 2,750 pounds.

The 12E was a commercial bonanza for Hiller. More of this version would be sold than all other civil models combined. This robust aircraft always did more, if anything, than the factory specifications called for. "The 12E was the Cadillac of the industry," remembers former Hiller employee Everett L. ("Curly") Barrick. "It was hell-for-stout, a workhorse—hand-finished, and every one off the assembly line had a personal touch."[17]

Hiller publicity photographs showed 12Es carrying huge utility poles, steel pipes, and other loads. "The machine could shake your teeth out," recalls Del Smith, "but it got the job done and it would fly anywhere under all kinds of weather conditions. It gave us the capacity to develop year-round work, which is what we needed to make our business viable."[18]

Taking advantage of the extra lifting capacity, Hiller in 1960 introduced a four-seat "station wagon" version of the 12E called the E4.[19] A 25-inch extension to the standard 12E's forward fuselage provided space for a separate pilot's seat ahead of bench-seating for three passengers. The basic airframe was otherwise unchanged except for a revised tail featuring an inverted-vee tailplane. Kits were available from the factory to convert standard 12Es to E4s. Both versions enjoyed such refinements to the Hiller line as dual carburetors, optional high-compression pistons that developed 340 hp, and

*E*leven Hiller employees weighing a total of 1,822 pounds hover aboard the Hiller UH-12D-1, prototype of the Hiller 12E series. Left to right: *secretary-treasurer Jim Dresher, director of flight test Phil Johnston, engineering staff assistant Bud Cheney, vice-president John Chadwick, flight test engineer Bob Jensen, Navy representative Lt. Cdr. Jack Caldwell, test pilot Dick Peck, project engineer Herb Moseley, assistant chief engineer (administrative) Bill Callery, marketing vice-president Bill Vincent, and test pilot Larry Lape.*

optional superchargers that maintained full-rated horsepower all the way up to 20,000 feet.

An extensive enlargement of Hiller's domestic and Canadian sales organization had been instituted at the start of 1959 to support these new machines. William Callery, Jr., formerly assistant chief engineer for administration, was appointed to the post of sales manager under Bill Vincent, vice-president in charge of sales and service. Reporting to Callery, in turn, was a new three-man staff of regional sales managers: Henry Eagle, Jr., eastern and central North America; Kirby Achee, the southern U.S.; and Fred Jamieson, the western states and provinces. Reflecting a substantial increase in Hiller Aircraft's commercial marketing effort, this restructuring paved the way for the 12E's remarkable success.

Other key personnel changes early in 1959 stemmed from a decision by Hiller's board of directors to elevate two employees to vice-presidential rank. Operations Division manager Joseph B. Black and Finance Division manager James T. Dresher became vice-presidents in charge of operations and finance, respectively. Joe Black had headed Hiller's manufacturing organization since 1955, arriving with considerable managerial experience gained in the aircraft industry and the Air Force. Arriving as corporate treasurer and secretary in 1956, Jim Dresher had come from Martin Aircraft in Baltimore, where he had held key contract, cost control, and corporate financial-planning posts.

Closing out a busy decade, Hiller Aircraft recorded sales of $16,211,624 in 1959. This brisk volume of business marked a

23 percent increase over the preceding year, although net income after taxes at $305,903 was actually slightly lower than for 1958 due to heavy write-offs of aircraft development costs. All of the company's $1.6 million long-term debt had been converted to capital stock or retired, however, and shareholder's equity rose by $1.32 to $9.61 per share. "We are confident the company's position in the industry was materially improved," President Stanley Hiller, Jr., therefore observed at a New York news conference in March 1960, "and that the future years will benefit from the heavy expenditures charged against 1959 profits."[20]

Although Hiller Aircraft's helicopter production and VTOL work was well known, a wide variety of interesting lesser efforts were overshadowed by the major programs. Hiller at the end of 1959 acquired North and Central American sales rights to the Bölkow Bo 102 Heli-Trainer, a West German helicopter training-aid providing students with realistic control movement and response; essentially a captive helicopter, the trainer was topped by a small rotor powered by a 40-hp engine. Another effort—this one developed in-house—was a self-propelled warehouse pallet called the GEM-JAK; a commercial spinoff of recent ground-effect machine (GEM) studies sponsored by the Army through the ONR, the GEM-JAK supported very heavy loads on a cushion of air. Yet other little-known company products ranged in size from knee-pad navigation plotters for fighter pilots to large ground-based radar antenna arrays.

A dramatic mountain rescue—more than twice as high as the Sierra Nevada rescue eleven years earlier which had

Construction of roads and dams in rough country is greatly facilitated by the rugged 12E. Operated by Evergreen Helicopters, a subsidiary of Evergreen International Airlines of McMinnville, Oregon, this 12E carries sand off a hilltop to a nearby construction site. Courtesy Evergreen.

A Hiller 12E returns a Luscombe
Model 8 (damaged in a forced landing)
to a Venezuelan airfield.

helped sales of the original Model 360—gave an unexpected boost to the Hiller 12E in the spring of 1960. On the weekend of 21–22 May, Link Luckett, operator of a helicopter charter service in Anchorage, Alaska, successfully rescued two mountain climbers, one with a broken leg, from the 18,000-foot level of Mt. McKinley. This was the highest-altitude helicopter rescue in history, and Luckett's six landings over two days were also the highest landings and takeoffs to date by *any* type of aircraft, by a margin of almost three thousand feet.

Responding immediately to a plea for help, Luckett flew his Hiller 12E to the expedition's base camp at the 10,200-foot level, where he removed its doors, seat cushions, and battery to save weight. The protection of arctic flying gear proving inadequate on his first rescue attempt, Luckett was forced to reinstall one of the doors to reduce the severe wind whistling through his helicopter.

With just ten gallons of fuel—enough for a half-hour's flight—Link Luckett climbed to 19,300 feet and descended into what he described as a "blue icy area with heavy snow cover" where the climbers were stranded.[21] After bringing them out one by one, Luckett returned repeatedly to collect their gear.

"Winds were turbulent and hard to predict from one moment to the next," the pilot reported. "Through the open cabin door I threw out about six smoke bombs during the course of the six landings at the 18,000-foot site."[22]

In addition to demonstrating the 12E's performance, Luckett's widely hailed rescue drove home the fact that, for once, commercial operators had beat the military to the punch; the Army had yet to add this latest Hiller to its inventory. Perhaps to disguise this fact, there would be no H-23E; the Army's first large order for 12Es in 1961 carried the designation OH-23G (the "O" suffix reflecting reclassification of the H-23 series as observation helicopters). The four-seat E4, thirty-three of which were eventually ordered, was further designated the OH-23F.

As a private venture, Hiller built and demonstrated an instrument-trainer version of the OH-23F in 1962 under the designation TH-23F. It had a new rotor system (described below) and three seats arranged to permit the simultaneous training of two students. One student flew from the front right seat (the instructor being to his left) while another observed from a central seat behind them. When time came to swap positions, the right seat slid back to facilitate changing places.

The Canadian Army's twenty-two CH-112s (12Es) entering service in 1961 proved so well-adapted to the rugged far North that Canada's Air Force also bought three CH-112s. Great Britain's Royal Navy, pleased with the HTE-2s it had received ten years earlier, found that the fourteen 12Es it bought in 1962 demonstrated an availability rate surpassing that of all its other helicopters, not to mention many of the fleet's fixed-wing aircraft.

Despite its excellence, the H-23 series was inevitably nearing the end of its life. Military sales were becoming ever more difficult for Hiller because Bell Helicopter, now with many government contracts to subsidize its operations, could under-

The Hiller E4, a four-seat "station wagon" version of the 12E, was introduced in 1960. A 25-inch extension provided space for a separate pilot's seat forward of bench seating for three passengers.

sell Hiller. A mid-1950s contract for a medium-size helicopter (initially called the XH-40) would alone eventually carry all of Bell's overhead; redesignated the HU-1, then UH-1 Iroquois, this was the ubiquitous "Huey" of Vietnam War fame.

"The only way we stayed in competition," Hiller later observed, "was to prove with the Army's own figures that the H-23s cost less to operate over a period of time; to show that ours was a lower total-cost program despite higher initial cost."[23]

For a time, the Army adopted a "directed procurement" specifying purchase of fixed quantities of trainers from both Bell and Hiller, an arrangement that continued until 1967 when its final order for OH-23s was placed. Altogether some 1,693 H-23s were built by Hiller for the U.S. Army over a span of almost two decades. Another eighty-six had been built for foreign governments under the terms of the Mutual Defense Assistance Program (MDAP).

If H-23 production was nearing an end, a large new military program was now on the horizon. In October 1960, the Navy—on behalf of the Army—solicited design proposals for a new-generation turbine-powered light observation helicopter (LOH). The potential volume of military sales of this new machine was so great as to guarantee the winner a preemptive share of the emerging civil market as well. The LOH competition—which was shaping up to be perhaps the biggest military helicopter contract ever issued—received top priority at Palo Alto as Hiller engineers threw themselves into design of an advanced new helicopter.

Anticipating this program, Hiller had for several years been sending engineers like Wayne Wiesner and Bud Cheney on extended tours of military bases to discuss requirements with hundreds of military personnel. By the time design work began in earnest, Hiller felt it knew what the Army wanted better than the Army did.

A radically different rotor developed for Hiller's LOH prototype was tested in 1961 on the H-23D-2, a second 12E prototype that had been set aside for this purpose. Lacking the distinctive Rotormatic paddles that had been the trademark of every other Hiller helicopter ever produced, the "L" rotor combined a Hamilton Standard stability-augmentation system (SAS) and new, wide-chord rotor blades with a high lift and an inertia that permitted a gross weight increase to a hefty 3,100 pounds. Constructed of stainless steel with weight-saving metal honeycomb trailing edges, these long-life blades gave a smoother ride, more solid control feel, and superior autorotation characteristics. The L rotor was offered commercially in 1963 on the Hiller 12E as the 12E-L.

In 1964, the 12E-L became the Hiller L3, and the E4 with the new rotor became the L4. Supercharged versions of each, the SL3 (a military version of which was proposed to the Royal Australian Air Force) and SL4, were available in 1965, the final year of helicopter production in Palo Alto. In 1962, Hiller had concluded an agreement with Pratt & Whitney of Canada for development of a Model 12 powered by a 500 shp PT6 turboshaft engine. This contract produced a single prototype designated the JL5.

*S*ubstitution of the high-inertia
"L" rotor developed for Hiller's light
observation helicopter gave rise to the
12E-L of 1964. The E4 with the new
rotor, which dispensed with the familiar
Rotormatic paddles, became the L4
illustrated here.

Another turbine installation was available from Soloy Conversions Ltd. of Chehalis, Washington. The UH12-J3 (a conversion of the standard 12E or E4) incorporated an Allison 250-C20B turboshaft power plant weighing 158 pounds and producing 420 shp. The Soloy conversion had in fact been developed by Hiller Aircraft, but the company had decided not to market it. Longtime Hiller helicopter operator Joe Soloy is today a legend in the commercial helicopter industry.

For operators desiring additional performance but unable to afford turbine power, Hiller also offered its customers the option of a turbocharged Lycoming piston engine. The turbo, which greatly increased altitude performance, paid for itself when a heavy load, altitude, and hot weather conspired to make life miserable for operators of helicopters with normally aspirated engines.

In March 1983, twenty-four years after it was built, a turbocharged Hiller 12E set a phenomenal altitude record of 27,900 feet. Flown by Terry Clark, an experienced pilot who had commanded helicopter gunships in Vietnam, the vintage Hiller demonstrated sustained cruise to capture official world class and U.S. national records for piston helicopters. Clark's helicopter was the prototype for a commercially marketed turbocharger retrofit intended to boost the performance of working Hillers. This Phoenix Conversion, as it is known, was developed by Calvin Hunt and is marketed by Craig Helicopters of Colorado.

There is an odd phenomenon in helicopter flight whereby the floor beneath one's seat appears to shrink as one climbs higher. Five miles up, Clark's perch offered little more psychological support than a postage stamp. He later characterized this unusual flight as "harder than any mission I ever flew in Vietnam."[24]

The stability augmentation system (SAS) required in Hillers with the L-rotor worked well, but its complexity and expense were simply not justified in a helicopter already as good as the 12E. Future production of this helicopter series—which would shift over the years to other locations—would concentrate on the standard 12E with Rotormatic paddles reinstated.

Another interesting use of the Rotormatic system in more recent years would further underscore its value: almost all radio-controlled gasoline-powered scale model helicopters—be they models of Sikorskys, Bells, Agustas, Bölkows, or whatever—require Hiller Rotormatic paddles for sufficient stability and control to fly. Without Hiller's patented paddles, model helicopter flight would probably not have been able to evolve parallel to radio-controlled model airplanes as a hobby.

Had the Army been receptive, Hiller might have built an odd-looking turbine-powered light helicopter called the CAMEL (Collapsible Airborne Military Equipment Lifter). Conceived in 1959, the Model 1091 was about the size of an H-23 but 400 pounds lighter. Its high back and open frame accommodated loads of all sizes and shapes weighing up to 1,500 pounds. Power was to be supplied by either a 250 shp Allison T63 or a 430 shp Boeing T60 turboshaft engine.

A full-size nonflying mock-up built in 1960 (under new model number 1094)

Designed for parachute delivery by USAF transport plane, the Hiller CAMEL (Collapsible Airborne Military Equipment Lifter) was easily assembled in the field without special tools. The proposed turbine-powered CAMEL, which combined H-23 and Hornet components, was never built. This photograph illustrates a company mock-up.

had a Hiller YH-32 Hornet windshield and overhead stick, the dynamic components (rotors, shafts, transmission, and controls) and tail boom of an H-23D, and the Rotorcycle's collapsibility. Six folded CAMELs could fit into the hold of a Lockheed C-130 at one time. The helicopter could be assembled by two men in six minutes. A civil version of the CAMEL (the acronym now reworded to Civil Aerial Multi-Purpose Equipment Lifter) was also proposed, but the program ended before construction of a flying prototype because of a decided lack of Army interest.

A major new development effort took to the air on 14 July 1961. Designated the Hiller Model Ten99, this six-place all-purpose helicopter was powered by a 500 shp Pratt & Whitney PT6 turboshaft engine flat-rated to 350 shp. No larger than the three-seat Hiller 12E, the Ten99 could in just minutes be smaller still for easy transport by cargo plane: the landing skids folded up and the tail cone came off with the removal of just a couple of bolts. With understandable pride, therefore, a Hiller promotional publication described the new machine as "the smallest big helicopter flying."[25]

With a gross weight of 3,500 pounds and a payload of more than a thousand pounds, the Ten99 was indeed a "big" helicopter in terms of utility. Wide side doors and clamshell rear doors greatly facilitated loading the boxy aircraft's capacious 100-cubic-foot cargo hold. Engine, transmission, and shafting, moreover, all sat atop the fuselage under a domed cowling instead of invading the interior space, as was universally the case with small helicopters. Although the

Ten99 first flew with Rotormatic paddles, an L-Rotor was soon fitted for improved performance.

The Ten99 was developed in anticipation of a major Marine Corps requirement for an assault support helicopter (ASH), to be procured by the Navy, from whom the Marines received their aircraft. Designed around the specified PT6 engine, the vehicle Hiller engineers came up with was ideally sized to address the mission of getting Marines and their equipment into tight corners rapidly and with great flexibility.

Despite war paint and dramatic promotional photographs showing the Ten99 in simulated action, however, the single prototype—civil registration N3776G—would remain a company demonstrator for want of a buyer. Canny marketing by the Bell Helicopter Company had convinced the Navy to select a version of the UH-1 Iroquois as its new assault support helicopter. Accordingly, the U.S. Marine Corps would soon be flying Hueys along with the Army and the Air Force.

The fact that the larger Huey was initially not eligible to compete in the ASH procurement had not stopped Bell. Believing it had a good vehicle for the assault support role, it first talked the Navy into waiving the requirement for use of the PT6 engine (this unit being too small to power the UH-1). The Fort Worth company then argued that volume production of the Huey—which promised to be built in far greater numbers than any previous helicopter—would bring prices down to acceptable levels despite larger size. The opportunity to get extra carrying capacity at no extra purchase cost appealed to Navy procure-

*W*ith overall dimensions comparable
to those of light helicopters, the Ten99
offered twice the passenger capacity, two
and a half times the usable cargo space,
and nearly double the payload.

ment officials, who proceeded to award the ASH contract to Bell.

Failure of the Hiller Ten99 to win this military contract placed its builder in a bind. Although business was booming and profits continued to climb, Hiller Aircraft had failed to achieve volume production of any new product since the introduction of the UH-12 series in the late 1940s. Although 12E orders currently constituted the largest peacetime backlog in the company's history, every Hiller employee knew that it could not continue forever.

Hiller had invested a great deal in the Ten99, which (like the inexpensive CAMEL before it) was financed entirely with company funds. After the UH-12 series itself, in fact, the Ten99 helicopter was the most expensive program yet pursued by Hiller Aircraft. The lack of military support dealt a double blow, since it also undermined plans to introduce an executive transport version of the Ten99 to the civil market. With club seating for four in an elegantly appointed interior separate from the cockpit, the civil Ten99—complete with folding work table to serve as a desk—had promised the privacy and utility of a small office.

If Hiller Aircraft were to survive, new sources of production were clearly needed. The failure of the Ten99— even by today's standards an excellent helicopter—underscored the realization that time was growing short. However successful the company's research and development programs, and however well its new prototypes flew, these things could not carry the company without a healthy base of volume manufacture.

Fortunately, if the early 1960s brought great challenge, they also offered unprecedented opportunity, for a potentially huge new military production program now lay on the horizon. The Army's forthcoming light observation helicopter (LOH) competition was tailor-made for the Hiller team, whose long experience building light helicopters for the Army gave it a clear edge over much of the rest of the aviation industry.

Therefore, though a lot of money had gone into the Ten99, much more still was now allocated to the Palo Alto team's entry for the landmark LOH competition. Behind the confident determination of Hiller's uniquely talented engineering staff, driving them to new heights, lay the knowledge that—like it or not—the very existence of Hiller Aircraft might depend on the success of the trim turbine helicopter now taking shape on their drawing boards.

Much was also happening on the business front, and by early 1964 it was obvious that association with ELTRA had become less desirable. Over time, the organization had evolved into a holding company with too many divisions in different fields all competing for its resources. It was evident to Stanley Hiller, moreover, that ELTRA would eventually be for sale.

To support the XC-142 and his other promising projects, Hiller needed to reposition his company more favorably. He discounted joining forces with Douglas, Lockheed, or any other aerospace giant because the sheer size difference alone threatened to deny Hiller Aircraft

Billionaire aviator Howard Hughes stands before his Hughes H-1 Racer in 1937. A quarter-century later, the reclusive Hughes would seek to establish himself as a helicopter manufacturer. His ill-advised effort cost him $90 million and would spell an end to Hiller Aircraft. Courtesy NASM/SI.

any measure of control over its own destiny.

Instead, Hiller settled upon Fairchild Stratos, the name since 1961 of the venerable Fairchild Engine and Airplane Company of Hagerstown, Maryland. It fit the bill nicely and—currently undervalued following years of lackluster management—it presented an attractive business opportunity. In addition to providing a new plateau of economic prowess, the association promised healthy diversification. In an arrangement proposed by Hiller, Fairchild bought the Palo Alto company from ELTRA on 5 May 1964.

During the negotiations, Stanley Hiller had begun purchasing stock with his own money to become the second largest Fairchild shareholder after Sherman Fairchild himself. He now took up duties as executive vice-president and board member of the combined company. Ed Bolton remained in Palo Alto as general manager of Fairchild's new Hiller Aircraft Division.

The restructured Maryland-based aircraft company further moved to acquire Republic Aviation on Long Island, New York. For continued product recognition, it had been decided during negotiations with Fairchild that the Hiller name would be retained. Accordingly, a now much-enlarged Fairchild Stratos officially became the Fairchild Hiller Corporation in November 1964.

Those shareholders who followed Hiller through Electric Autolite/ELTRA to Fairchild now saw another major increase in their investment. For Stanley Hiller

himself, the repositioning gave newfound muscle to his company, poising it at the brink of a higher level of capability. The future had never looked so bright nor horizons so wide.

That the Hiller company would soon cease to exist as a distinct and vibrant entity within Fairchild Hiller, and that he himself would leave aviation for new and more profitable business ventures, was the last thing on Stanley Hiller's mind as he celebrated his fortieth birthday in his Washington, D.C., home. An immediate cause of these unanticipated changes—and of a major upheaval in the helicopter industry as a whole—were the bizarre actions of noted billionaire oil-industry heir Howard Robard Hughes, Jr.

Intent upon buying his way into the helicopter business, Howard Hughes would subvert the Army's milestone light observation helicopter procurement in order to win the competition. In the process, he would throw a balanced, healthy industry into turmoil. Bribery, industrial espionage, false bidding, and betrayal of the public trust—as brought to light in a 1967 congressional investigation—were his tools in this high-stakes theft.

Hughes's well-documented actions may have been the immediate instrument of Hiller Aircraft's demise, but other factors—both internal and external—helped set the stage. In fact, a complex concatenation of events would conspire to end the flowering of vertical-flight creativity that had been Hiller Aircraft.

End of an Era

The future indeed had never looked so bright for Hiller Aircraft as when it joined forces with Fairchild in 1964. The amalgamation of the two companies placed Hiller in a position of newfound strength across a broad spectrum of the industry as a manufacturer of both rotary-wing and fixed-wing aircraft.

The combined interests of the new entity were impressive. On the Hiller side, the Vought-Hiller-Ryan XC-142A VTOL transport aircraft was almost ready to fly; unlike the one-of-a-kind X-18 research plane, the five C-142 prototypes had production potential. Equally important, Hiller's OH-5A prototype was already in the air and appeared likely to win the Army's light observation helicopter (LOH) competition. The Palo Alto assembly lines were still busy: demand for Model UH-12 commercial helicopters ran at record levels, and current military contracts—despite the fact that the Raven was nearing the end of its production life—gave Hiller its largest peacetime H-23 backlog in company history. Finally, the possibility still remained that government sponsorship might at last make the Hiller tip-powered flying crane a reality.

On the Fairchild side, there was license production of the Fokker F-27 Friendship turboprop airliner and of Fairchild Hiller's stretched FH-227 version. The company was also gearing up to build under license the Swiss-designed Turbo-Porter, a single-turbine-engine STOL (short-takeoff-and-landing) aircraft.

With the further acquisition of Republic Aviation, Fairchild Hiller had the F-105 Thunderchief program which, although the fighter-bomber itself was out of production, would continue to garner Air Force spare parts and support contracts throughout the Vietnam War. Republic was currently building F-4 Phantom II empennages as a subcontractor to McDonnell, and it was working on several highly classified government projects including the stainless-steel XF-103, a research-oriented fighter-bomber intended to fly at Mach four. Bringing Republic into the fold also brought to Fairchild Hiller the prized talents of noted designer Alexander Kartveli. And last, acquiring the Long Island company brought one-third ownership of Fokker in Holland.

Hiller began transferring production from Palo Alto to Hagerstown in 1965. Consolidating manufacture under one roof rather than operating two plants at lower capacity yielded a more competitive

*F*irst flown on 26 January 1963, the
Hiller OH-5A combined rugged
construction and excellent performance.
Courtesy NASM/SI.

cost factor and made good business sense. "A difficult decision even to think about, let alone make," as Hiller described it in 1967, this transfer was nevertheless essential and unavoidable.[1] Plans called for R&D engineering activities alone to remain at the Willow Road complex. At this time, therefore, most of Hiller Aircraft's work force either had to relocate to Maryland or leave the company. Many longtime employees opted to retire in northern California.

Ironically, combining with Fairchild had hardly lessened the singular importance to company fortunes of the LOH competition. Before acquiring Hiller, Fairchild Stratos had been plagued with excess plant capacity and a paucity of aircraft production; the company as a whole now looked eagerly to its new Hiller Aircraft Division for needed business.

Winning the LOH competition in fact remained critical to the survival of the Hiller division. With nothing comparable to Bell's Huey program to carry its overhead and maintain its financial health, it badly needed LOH production to remain competitive. Were Hiller to lose to Bell or Hughes, the other declared finalists, and were Hiller to try without military funding to sell its new helicopter on the civil market, it would find it impossible to compete on a cost basis for very long with whichever company had won.

Hiller Aircraft's lack of success over the preceding decade to generate new volume-production programs had led to this all-or-nothing impasse, a dangerous juncture at which every aircraft manufacturer has found itself at one time or another. Production of the Army's venerable H-23, moreover, was drawing to an end, and civil 12E sales certainly did not represent a sales base of sufficient size for longevity. For better or for worse, the Hiller division's fate rode squarely on the LOH. Auspiciously, however, the Fairchild Hiller's LOH entry had already been judged the winner of the competition's rigorous technical evaluation. At the close of 1964, it was hard to see how the graceful OH-5A could lose out on the final decision.

But Fairchild Hiller was not destined to win the LOH competition. In a fascinating instance of a procurement gone awry, this milestone in light helicopter development would fall prey to the unethical scheme of a bedridden eccentric high atop a Las Vegas casino. Howard Hughes's weapons of subversion (alliteratively summarized as "babes, booze, and bribes")[2] would wreak havoc within the helicopter industry and would deny to Hiller Aircraft sufficient production volume to survive.

Howard Hughes, Jr., was, of course, sole heir to the Hughes Tool Company fortune. The Texas-based company—manufacturer of a drill bit invented by Howard Hughes, Sr., in 1908 which had revolutionized the petroleum industry—provided Hughes, Jr., with access to more than a billion dollars to pursue his interests. Enigmatic and flamboyant, Hughes dabbled in filmmaking, but aviation was his first love. A noted flier in his earlier years, he set records including a whirlwind flight around the world in 1938. He also built and tested military aircraft as described below, and he controlled Trans World Airlines for fifteen years.

The Howard Hughes of the 1960s was

a far different person, although the society-page glamor lingered in the public mind. He had become pathologically eccentric and self-serving, running his business empire from his bed. He was no longer seen in public, and his self-imposed exile masked a progressive deterioration of both his physical and mental health. Bad investments had reduced his personal fortune to below a billion dollars. Hughes had never been a good businessman. If people generally thought otherwise, it was largely the product of his lifelong obsession with his own carefully cultivated image. His constant "fine tuning" of public perceptions—he would plant stories, take detractors to task, and otherwise promote a public persona often at odds with reality—was so effective that to this day few people are disposed to think ill of him.

The light observation helicopter competition announced in October 1960 was clearly strategic, for the volume of military sales it promised was potentially so great as to guarantee the winner a preemptive share of the emerging civil light-turbine-helicopter market. In fact, it would probably be the biggest helicopter contract yet issued by the U.S. Government. As such, it caught Hughes's eye as a golden opportunity.

Hughes saw in this competition perhaps his last chance to establish himself in the cherished role of aircraft manufacturer. His previous attempts to gain a foothold in the industry had been totally unsuccessful: On the eve of World War II, Hughes had failed to interest the Army Air Corps in either a fighter version of his H-1 racer or a wooden bomber called the D-2. During the war,

obsessed with leaving his mark on history, he undertook two ambitious projects which were both completed too late for wartime service, even had a need existed for them. The Hughes XF-11, a twin-engine photo-reconnaissance aircraft designed without regard for military requirements, flew in July 1946 and was destroyed in a crash that left Hughes badly injured. The second wartime project was the wooden HK-1 Hercules flying boat—nicknamed the *Spruce Goose*—which Hughes lifted briefly from the water just once to a height of seventy feet in November 1947.

Widely hailed by a glamor-hungry public, this hop served to defuse a 1947 Senate investigation into Hughes Aircraft's singularly poor record among America's wartime defense contractors. The War Investigating Committee wanted to know why the celebrated aviator had so very little to show for some $40 million in public funds he had received during the war.[3] After the giant Hughes-Kaiser machine lifted above the Pacific Ocean, public opinion sided firmly with Hughes who had portrayed himself throughout as the innocent victim of governmental persecution. Without reaching a determination, the congressional inquiry came to a halt.

By the early 1950s, although no longer building aircraft, the Hughes Aircraft Company had become a major component of the growing military-industrial complex as a supplier of missiles and electronic fire-control systems. The company did well when left to its own devices; when Hughes involved himself in its running, however, it was a different story. His inept meddling in 1953 precipitated an exodus of key corporate officers, who founded Thompson-Ramo-Wooldridge (TRW) and Litton Industries, and further provoked the threat of mass resignation by the company's scientific advisory council. Perceiving a threat to national security in the growing chaos, the Department of Defense issued an ultimatum: Howard Hughes would desist from all participation in the running of Hughes Aircraft or all military contracts would be summarily canceled. Since so drastic an action would have spelled an end to the company, Hughes had no choice but to accede.

Hughes's LOH proposal would come not from Hughes Aircraft, therefore, but rather from the Hughes Tool Company's Aircraft Division, which confusingly enough was collocated with the much-larger Hughes Aircraft at Culver City, California. Sole owner of this tiny entity, Hughes took pains this time to conceal the fact that he personally was in control. At that time, the Aircraft Division was building the Hughes 269 two-seat piston helicopter then being evaluated by the Army as the TH-55A.[4] Having operated at a loss ever since its creation, the Aircraft Division enjoyed a singularly poor reputation in the industry. A former Lockheed executive brought on board to help market the Hughes LOH characterized the Aircraft Division as "a lousy, inept operation."[5]

Still unable to buy its own aircraft under the terms of the 1948 Key West Accord, the Army asked the Navy to administer the procurement. In January 1961, twelve manufacturers—some of whom had never before built a helicopter—submitted seventeen design proposals for consideration by the two services. In the end, the Navy chose Hiller Aircraft because its "design was the only one acceptable from a technical viewpoint," while the Army selected only Hiller's and Bell's entries.[6] In accordance with past Army practice, these experienced rivals (Hiller to date had built 60 percent of the Army's light helicopters; Bell had built 40 percent in addition to larger types)[7] alone got contracts for the construction of prototypes.

Its proposal rejected, the Hughes Tool Company's Aircraft Division was now firmly out of the running. Howard Hughes, however, was unwilling to concede the fact. At his urging, Hughes vice-president (and former helicopter test pilot) Albert W. Bayer—who boasted of extensive personal contacts within the Army's most senior staff—sought special favor in violation of an existing ban on lobbying. At Bayer's covert instigation, General Clyde D. Eddleman, then acting chief of staff, ordered the selection board to reconvene on a Saturday in an extraordinary session from which, strangely enough, the Navy and Marine Corps were excluded. Brigadier General Clifton F. von Kann, director of Army aviation and another of Bayer's high-level "friends," then spearheaded reconsideration of the Hughes proposal. Peculiarly—but perhaps not surprisingly, in view of the circumstances—no minutes were taken.

This meeting remains infamous in the annals of military procurement. When it ended, the vote on the Hughes proposal had been reversed; in an unprecedented and highly abnormal situation, three helicopter types rather than the usual two

Lighter than its rivals in the Army's light observation helicopter (LOH) competition, the Hughes OH-6A was faster but less rugged than the Bell OH-4A or the Hiller OH-5A. Courtesy NASM/SI.

were now to be constructed and tested. On 13 November 1961, the Army awarded contracts for five each Bell OH-4As (serial nos. 62-4201/4205), Hiller OH-5As (62-4206/4210), and Hughes OH-6As (62-4211/4215). All three types were to be powered by the Allison T63 turboshaft engine, developed under Army auspices specifically for such use.

The first Hiller OH-5A (company Model FH-1100) flew on 26 January 1963. From the start, this sleek turbine-powered thoroughbred looked and acted like a winner. Buoyed by its first-place selection, Hiller was fully confident that it had the best machine. The OH-5 featured sliding rear doors that (unlike the OH-6's hinged civil-type doors) could be opened in flight. Less obvious to the eye but even more important, it had Hiller's very safe high-inertia L-rotor, as well as skid landing gear mounted on longitudinal torque tubes. By deforming in a crash or hard landing, these tubes would absorb impact forces to spare both the helicopter and its occupants. As testing began, Hiller could only hope that the Army appreciated such features and understood what was truly desirable in the multipurpose light observation role.

It soon became alarmingly evident that the Hughes team had access to highly privileged information. First, Hughes knew that the Army planned an initial order of 1,000 aircraft over three years, valuable knowledge in computing prices. Second, Hughes knew that the competition would be between itself and Hiller; although no formal announcement would be made for some time, the Bell entry—pronounced "highest in cost and lowest

in military capability" by the Army—had been eliminated.[8] Third, Hughes knew both Hiller's proposal price and specific cost data, which information could only have come from confidential financial reports Hiller had submitted at the request of the Army.

Fired by Hughes Tool Company vice-president Rea E. Hopper after an unsuccessful power play, Alfred Bayer let this bombshell drop during an October 1964 meeting with Stanley Hiller, during which Bayer unsuccessfully sought employment with the latter. After the meeting at Hiller's Washington office, recalled Hiller vice-president Warren Rockwell, "Mr. Hiller came out and he was visibly shaken, actually white."[9] The Palo Alto company immediately pressed for an official investigation of the leak. After several months, the Army announced that it had failed to find any evidence of wrongdoing, either within its own ranks or by the Hughes Tool Company.

The Hughes helicopter itself was smaller, lighter, and faster than Hiller's or Bell's. Overall, the Army liked its diminutive size, although one general who was a rated helicopter pilot noted that the OH-6A was "very light and probably would not stand up to service usage."[10] Lieutenant Colonel Samuel R. Boyer, the Army's liaison to the Navy during selection of the LOH, also voiced concerns about the "thin-gauge materials on the aircraft, the very lightweight approach taken."[11] The OH-6A was so lightly built, in fact, that the Army had to reclassify the competition from military specification to less rugged FAA certification

A test pilot prepares to start the fourth
of five OH-4A prototypes built by Bell
in Fort Worth, Texas. Courtesy Bell
Helicopter Textron.

standards for it to qualify. Bell and Hiller, in contrast, had designed to military specifications from the outset.

Because the OH-6A employed the lightweight rotor-blade approach Hughes had introduced on its Model 269, it featured poor autorotation characteristics and was manifestly less safe than its competitors. As stated by Colonel Boyer, "the Navy dropped the Hughes entry out . . . because of the autorotative characteristics of the Hughes machine. It is a low inertia rotor system, and it has autorotative characteristics—I am a helicopter pilot myself—that I don't like. You come down like a streamlined brick."[12]

Aggravating both these problems, the Army, having opted for the lightest vehicle, then quixotically proceeded to demand that the gross vehicular weight be upped to allow it to perform its stated missions. Hughes complied with an increase from 2,100 to 2,400 pounds. When the Army then asked for 2,700 pounds (the Hiller OH-5A's gross weight was 2,750 pounds) for additional equipment to increase utility to the level of Bell's and Hiller's helicopters, the FAA denied certification on the grounds of safety. Referring to the Hughes OH-6A, FAA flight-test specialist Donald Armstrong told congressional investigators, "We have data to show it cannot be certificated at that weight. . . . It would be at the expense of compliance with present civil airworthiness requirements in both controllability and, I believe, performance."[13]

Although smaller, the Hughes OH-6A was roughly as costly to produce as the Hiller OH-5A and slightly less expensive than Bell's OH-4A. Minus engine, radios,

and other government-furnished equipment, that meant a price of almost $30,000 per aircraft. Howard Hughes sat in bed agonizing endlessly over how much to bid per helicopter to win the fixed-price Army contract. He knew that the Army had already eliminated the Bell entry, although that fact had yet to be made public. Hiller was the competitor to beat, and Hughes was obsessed with doing so. Since he himself planned to resort to unscrupulous measures to secure the contract, he had mistakenly convinced himself his competitors would do the same.

In the end, desperate not to lose, Howard Hughes bid an absurdly low $19,860 per helicopter. Even Rea Hopper, the Aircraft Division's general manager, was forced to concede that it was "not really a good figure; this is not the way people are supposed to price things, I don't think."[14] Less charitable assessments were heard elsewhere in the industry, one example being the vehement reaction of Hiller LOH contracts manager William D. Rollnick: "They were totally out of their minds."[15]

Howard Hughes had now embarked upon an ill-advised and highly unethical "buy-out." The term refers to winning a contract through false low pricing. Typically in a buy-out scheme, once the other contenders have been eliminated, the winner—who has established himself as the sole supplier—raises his price to the government to recoup his initial losses and to reap additional profits at public expense.

Subversion of the procurement process by Generals von Kann and Eddleman had been possible because of the disorganized state of Army aviation. Further evidence of confusion within that service was now at hand. Failing to question the patently unreasonable price, the Army awarded the LOH contract to the Aircraft Division of the Hughes Tool Company on 26 May 1965. Hughes had now committed himself to building 714 helicopters at an estimated loss per machine of $11,000, representing a personal loss to him of almost $8 million. The Army's first installment of its order called for eighty-eight machines.

Because U.S. involvement in Vietnam was escalating rapidly, meanwhile, the Army placed a separate order for 121 more OH-6s to be produced concurrently with the original 88 machines. Eager to recoup, Howard Hughes raised his price for these additional helicopters—which were not part of the order for 714—to $55,927 each, a stunning price increase of 282 percent. Desperate attempts by a now-alarmed Army to negotiate with its sole supplier brought the price down only to $49,500 (still almost $30,000 more per aircraft than before), which was as far as Hughes was willing to come down.

The Army agreed and asked Congress for supplemental funds to purchase additional Hughes helicopters. So great was congressional consternation over the price disparity, however, that the Army immediately tried to withdraw its request, but it was too late to avoid acute embarrassment. Congressman L. Mendel Rivers, chairman of the House Armed Services Committee, had already directed his Subcommittee for Special Investigations to conduct a formal inquiry. Much of the information presented in this chapter in fact came to light during this investigation which, at its conclusion in 1967, focused withering criticism on the Army for its mishandling of the procurement process.

A clause in the original LOH contract permitted the Army to order up to half again more helicopters at the original price, should it so desire. With American lives being lost in Vietnam for want of light-turbine helicopters, this option was fully invoked for 357 more Hughes OH-6As. A horrified Howard Hughes now realized that he suddenly stood to lose half again more than he had anticipated.

Production at Culver City, meanwhile, was in serious trouble. Disorganized, badly structured, and woefully unprepared for mass production, Hughes Tool Company's Aircraft Division was turning out a mere trickle of Army helicopters instead of the stream so urgently needed. Hughes had committed his company to delivering 88 OH-6As in fiscal year 1965, 168 in 1966, and 458 in 1967, making the total of 714. He was hardly off to an auspicious start: by the end of fiscal year 1965, his company had delivered exactly 12 helicopters.

"There wasn't a blessed thing going on when we sent our people out [to Culver City] and they took pictures of . . . what should have been the production line," observed Congressman Porter Hardy, Jr., the subcommittee chairman. "And anybody with two grains of sense examining those pictures would have known it was impossible for this delivery schedule to be met."[16]

To Hughes's dismay, having exercised its option for more helicopters under the old price, the Army—at the insistence of

Congress—canceled its order for 121 additional OH-6As and went elsewhere to buy its helicopters. This about-face astounded military and industry observers alike; by long tradition, once a manufacturer became the supplier of an article of military equipment, whatever it might be, it would remain the supplier as long as the military continued to use that item. Initially unwilling to depart from this sacrosanct if unofficial policy, the Army only with great reluctance yielded to intense congressional pressure to do so.

Fairchild Hiller, meantime, had tooling in place to produce new LOHs, since it had decided to bring a civil version of the OH-5A to market. Granted FAA certification on 20 July 1964, and rolled out on 3 June 1966, the Fairchild Hiller FH-1100 was the first American light turbine helicopter to reach the commercial marketplace. If the OH-5A's chances had been good before, they were excellent now: relocating helicopter production to the Hagerstown factory, where there were other assembly lines to defray overhead costs, meant that the OH-5A now cost some $4,000 less to build than would previously have been the case.

Texas-based Bell Helicopter was also bringing a civil version of its LOH entry—revised with a simpler and lighter fuselage—to market as the Bell Model 206 JetRanger. Tooling was already in place, and it would be a simple matter to turn civilian JetRangers back into military machines. Bell needed no encouragement to jump at this unprecedented second chance.

But with everything to gain and nothing to lose, Fairchild Hiller refused to

bid this second time around. The reason lay in differences between Fairchild Hiller president Edward G. Uhl and executive vice-president Stanley Hiller. Disagreement between the two men—the latter also the company's second-largest stockholder—centered on two issues: how to deal with the military, and whether to continue commercial production.

It had been agreed during Fairchild Hiller's formation that Edward Uhl would concentrate on the internal running of the company while Stanley Hiller would attend to external affairs, an arrangement summarized at the time by the informal titles "Mr. Inside" and "Mr. Outside." One of Hiller's first tasks in the latter role was to convince Pentagon officials that troubled Republic Aviation—its F-105 Thunderchief then had a poor operational record—would, under Fairchild Hiller management, again be a credible supplier of military aircraft.

That Uhl had long-standing difficulties dealing with the military was a matter of record, and so Hiller's hard-won experience in procurement matters was needed. Of the two men, ironically, it was Uhl and not Hiller who harbored ill feelings toward the U.S. Army for permitting Howard Hughes to steal the LOH contract from Fairchild Hiller. Uhl's resultant antipathy toward the U.S. Army ran counter to an otherwise strong preference for military production over civil, for Uhl believed that Fairchild Hiller should get out of building commercial aircraft altogether.

Hiller disagreed strongly on both counts. Already looking forward to the second chance to build LOHs he knew must inevitably come, he also believed

Rated superior to the Hughes and Bell machines, Hiller's LOH entry missed two chances to be the Army's light turbine helicopter. The sliding rear doors of this civilian FH-1100 hint at its military origins.

there were many commercial opportunities for the company. His attempts to work toward these goals were repeatedly blunted, however, by apparent disinclination on the part of the company president. Sherman Fairchild, who might have acted to resolve this stalemate, instead chose not to involve himself directly in the running of the company.

With other challenges and business interests to pursue, Stan Hiller decided that one year of frustration with little to show for the effort was enough. Furthermore, the Hiller family missed the West Coast and felt it was time to return. Accordingly, at age forty (a stage in life often bringing change) Hiller prepared to move back to California with his wife and two growing boys.

He took satisfaction, nonetheless, in surveying the company he was leaving behind. With the Fairchild association, Hiller Aircraft now enjoyed a new capability and unprecedented opportunities. Better still, healthy corporate diversity had been achieved. Diversified operation was one element Hiller had worked long and hard to put in place, in addition to fulfilling his responsibility to shareholders, and establishing lines of development to provide for the future well-being of the company. Even if the end of the line was in sight for the Model 12E and OH-23G, the Palo Alto company had brought to Fairchild a huge backlog of orders, well over 600, for these helicopters.

And three Hiller projects were underway at Fairchild to provide for future business. The first was a new tip-propulsion effort involving the mounting of Williams turbojets on an L-Rotor-equipped HOE-1 Hornet, a test program Hiller had recently proposed to the Navy; that it had been well received by that service suggested that Hiller's tip-turbine flying crane program was still alive. The second was Gerhard Sissingh's "desensitized rotor," a possible next-generation approach to high-speed helicopter flight. The third, of course, was the OH-5/FH-1100, for Hiller knew that it was just a question of time before the Army, under pressure from Congress, solicited a new round of LOH bidding.

In Stanley Hiller's considered judgment, the time had clearly come to move on, and he fully expected that the company would continue to support these three major undertakings in his absence. "It seemed we had done everything we wanted," he said of his aircraft company and its activities. "While we hadn't succeeded in some projects, we had built up the company and made our stockholders a good return."[17]

Although this next entrepreneurial phase was not deliberately planned, Stanley Hiller had embarked upon a new career as a fixer of troubled corporations. Demanding no payment unless he succeeded, and spurning the "golden parachutes" often accorded top executives as protection against failure, he would spend the coming decades channeling his energies and abilities into "repairing" ailing businesses.

The corporations Hiller has since reshaped are all leaders of their respective industries, with sales ranging from hundreds of millions of dollars up into the billions. Most are Fortune 500 companies; all had suffered from the common malady of years of indifferent or poor management. Without divisive restructurings, Hiller—as chairman of the board or chief executive officer—and a few key associates restore these businesses to solid financial health before moving on to repeat the process at other troubled companies. These turnarounds are performed amicably at the request of the ailing companies' boards of directors.

In an era marked by liquidations, work-force decimation, and other manipulative strategies too often intent upon looting, Hiller engages only in constructive rebuilding and growth. He is philosophically opposed to participation in hostile takeovers or situations involving excessive debt leverage, and he eschews "quick-fix" measures that produce short-term profits at the expense of long-term health and growth-generating capital investment.

Hailed as one of corporate America's premier "fixers," Hiller has achieved an unbroken record of successful turnarounds since leaving aviation. The list of his involvements includes such industry giants as Baker International, Reed Tool, Bekins, and York International. "It's not any one million-dollar fix," Hiller says simply of his methods. "It's a whole bunch of thousand-dollar fixes."[18]

In a twist of fate that might hold elements of poetic justice, Stanley Hiller engineered the acquisition of an ailing Hughes Tool Company in 1987, years after Howard Hughes's death. As retired chairman of Baker International, an oil-tool industry giant he had helped shape, Hiller orchestrated the successful merger of the two companies into a profitable new corporate entity known as Baker-Hughes, with Baker management in full control.

Meanwhile, the Army's request for new bids for a light observation helicopter arrived in Maryland while Stanley Hiller was in California. Left to his own devices in Hagerstown, President Edward Uhl, still angry over the mishandling of the first round of bidding, resolved never to do business with the Army. Despite the urgings of his staff, Uhl steadfastly refused to participate in this second round of helicopter procurement.

Chief financial officer and second-in-command, James T. Dresher, a veteran of Hiller Aircraft, on his own initiative worked up a solid proposal for last-minute submittal should Uhl be persuaded to relent. Dresher argued that there was nothing to lose and everything to gain from submittal. As the deadline approached, however, it became ever more certain that the contest would be between Bell and Hughes alone. Fairchild Hiller simply would not participate.

In Las Vegas, meanwhile, a stricken Howard Hughes now faced the fact that in 1968 he was losing a whopping $62,000 on every helicopter he was compelled to build. Production speed-up costs, unrealistic manufacture estimates, and his original decision to underbid accounted for this unbelievable total. The only good news for Hughes—something that further appalled and dismayed Congress—was the Army's curious failure to specify, or even provide for, late charges in the LOH contract.

Trapped in a tight dilemma, Hughes once again agonized over how much to bid per helicopter. Too high a price this time around would lose him the Army's business and with it any hope of recovering part of his lost millions (Hughes no longer entertained hopes of easy profit). Bidding low enough to be certain of winning, on the other hand, would obligate him to extremely long-term production at an untenable loss. And the Hughes Tool Company—that seemingly inexhaustible money machine—was by now hard-pressed to support his escalating deficits.

Always quick to blame others and chronically unable to make decisions, the former billionaire now railed at his employees as he vacillated right up to the deadline. At the eleventh hour he entered a bid of $59,700 per OH-6 helicopter, only to learn on 10 March 1968 that Bell had underbid him to land a $123 million contract for 2,200 LOHs (designated OH-58 in Vietnam service).

Ironically, the bid sitting on Jim Dresher's desk in Hagerstown was lower than either Bell's or Hughes's. Had it been submitted, the OH-5 and its FH-1100 civilian counterpart would have been built in the thousands rather than the hundreds. But for this costly mistake, the Fairchild Hiller Corporation of Hagerstown, Maryland, might still be in business today.

Fully two more years would pass before the Hughes Tool Company's Aircraft Division fulfilled its existing military contracts, after which Hughes himself confronted a sickening truth: his unscrupulous attempt to corner the light-turbine helicopter market had reduced his personal fortune by $90 million. Only one advantage had accrued to an unrepentant Hughes: the fact that he had lost rather than profited, plus his popular image, had spared him prosecution.

In all probability, Hughes never gave much thought to the profoundly destructive consequences of his scheme gone sour. Uncounted lives were lost because U.S. forces in Vietnam failed to receive their desperately needed LOHs. The Army, which engaged in direct military aircraft procurement for the first time since 1942 to purchase the OH-6, lost credibility badly needed to support future programs. And Hiller Aircraft ceased to exist as a corporate entity. The Willow Road plant was closed in February 1966.

The greater public was perhaps unaware that the pioneering company, for two decades a builder of wondrous flying machines, had ceased to be. Among the ranks of helicopter pilots, however, it was a different story, and in aeronautical engineering circles, and throughout the world where lives had been touched—or even saved—by Hiller helicopters. There one heard words of regret and loss, for the helicopter and vertical-flight industry was stronger for the contributions of Hiller Aircraft.

At its peak in the early 1960s, the Hiller payroll numbered only some 2,000 employees. That this remarkable company offered its workers something unique is attested to by the fact that, as of this writing, hundreds of former Hiller employees still congregate each fall in annual reunions. During these gatherings, they recall the challenges and excitement of a unique work environment that Stanley Hiller himself inspired.

"It was quite like family," states Rose Lesslie, one of a number of women who,

*A*n aerial photograph of Hiller Aircraft in the early 1960s shows the tremendous growth that took place over fifteen years. Compare this view with the 1948 photograph on page 46.

189 End of an Era

in the "Rosie-the-Riveter" tradition established in World War II, worked at Hiller in the 1950s and 1960s. "We were very attached to each other, to the company, and to Stan Hiller. We were very loyal to him and had tremendous respect for him. He would come down to the work areas and speak to us, calling us by our first names."[19]

Conversations at the reunions inevitably touch upon pride of production, to an awareness of top-quality workmanship in every flying machine—conventional or exotic—ever rolled or carried out the factory door. One need only ask company veterans like Al Hutain, the former curator of the Hiller Aircraft Museum, or Curly Barrick, who restored the museum's gleaming Hiller 360.

The museum holds Hiller Aircraft's tangible legacy. Whether from a sense of history or from the singular esprit of technological challenges met and conquered, Stanley Hiller over the years preserved prototypes and production examples of his company's aircraft,

engines, and other products. As of this writing, the collection of the Hiller Museum is temporarily housed in Redwood City, California. This unique collection will soon join other Bay Area aviation artifacts being restored or replicated under Hiller's auspices for display in northern California's San Mateo County.

The Hiller Aircraft Company was a true industry pioneer. During its remarkable twenty-five years it ushered into being significant new technologies, beginning with the all-metal rotor blade, which have since become the industry standard. Although isolated and denied the advantages accorded other early helicopter builders, the small Palo Alto company flourished, sparked by the working philosophy of its founder and by the exuberant force of sheer creativity displayed by its team of personnel as it explored a broad spectrum of vertical flight possibilities.

Frank Coffyn said it best: it *was* like the Wright brothers all over again.

The Hiller/NASA recovery vehicle, formally proposed in 1965, was designed to retrieve spent 200-ton Saturn V moon booster first stages as they descended by parachute. Had it been built, this enormous tip-jet-powered helicopter would have had a rotor 300 feet in diameter and a gross weight of one million pounds.

This Hiller lift package, mounted atop a mobile test rig at Moffett Field, contains six pulse reactors. The side panel of this lift package is open, as are folding doors at top which permit the pulse reactors to extend upright for use.

Exploiting the muscle of the remarkable 12E, California's Pacific Gas & Electric uses Hillers in 1960 to transport 45-foot utility poles weighing over 900 pounds.

Appendix A

Specifications and Performance of Hiller Aircraft

Hiller 360 1948

Length (fuselage): 26 ft 6 in   8.08 m
Width (fuselage): 5 ft 0 in   1.52 m
Height: 9 ft 6 in   2.89 m
Rotor diameter: 35 ft 0 in   10.67 m

Empty weight: 1,432 lb   660 kg
Gross weight: 2,247 lb   1,020 kg

Top speed: 84 mph   134 km/h
Cruise speed: 76 mph   122 km/h
Initial rate of climb: 717 fpm   220 m/min
Absolute ceiling: 13,000 ft   3,048 m

Range: 210 mi   336 km
Fuel capacity: 27 U.S. gal   102 l

Power plant(s): Franklin 6V4-178-B33 six-cylinder horizontally opposed fan-cooled piston engine rated at 178 hp

Role/configuration: Three-seat light commercial helicopter

Hiller 12A/Army H-23A/Navy HTE-1 1950

Length: 26 ft 6 in   8.08 m
Width (fuselage): 5 ft 0 in   1.52 m
Height: 9 ft 6 in   2.89 m
Rotor diameter: 35 ft 0 in   10.67 m

Empty weight: 1,435 lb   660 kg
Empty weight (Army): 1,610 lb   685 kg
Gross weight: 2,400 lb   1,020 kg

Top speed: 84 mph   134 km/h
Cruise speed: 76 mph   122 km/h
Initial rate of climb: 400 fpm   220 m/min
Absolute ceiling: 10,000 ft   3,048 m

Range: 210 mi   336 km
Fuel capacity: 27 U.S. gal   102 l

Power plant(s): Franklin 6V4-178-B33 six-cylinder horizontally opposed 178 hp piston engine

Role/configuration: Three-seat commercial/military helicopter; used primarily by Army in air-evacuation role and by Navy as a trainer

Hiller 12-B/Army H-23B/Navy HTE-2 1952

Length: 26 ft 6 in 8.08 m
Width (fuselage): 5 ft 0 in 1.52 m
Height: 9 ft 10 in 3.00 m
Rotor diameter: 35 ft 0 in 10.67 m

Empty weight: 1,568 lb 711 kg
Empty weight (Army): 1,740 lb 790 kg
Gross weight: 2,500 lb 1,135 kg

Top speed: 84 mph 134 km/h
Cruise speed: 70 mph 112 km/h
Initial rate of climb: 770 fpm 235 m/min
Absolute ceiling: 9,400 ft 2,867 m

Range: 135 mi 216 km
Fuel capacity: 28 U.S. gal 106 l

Power plant(s): Franklin 6V4-200-C33 six-cylinder horizontally opposed piston engine rated at 200 hp

Role/configuration: Three-seat light commercial helicopter; light military training and (with side-mounted litters) air-evacuation helicopter; more rugged and powerful than previous models

HOE-1/YH-32 1953

Length: 12 ft 9 in 3.89 m
Width (fuselage): 3 ft 9 in 1.14 m
Height: 7 ft 10 in 2.38 m
Rotor diameter: 23 ft 0 in 7.00 m

Empty weight: 536 lb 243 kg
Gross weight: 1,080 lb 489 kg

Top speed: 80 mph 128 km/h
Cruise speed: 69 mph 111 km/h
Initial rate of climb: 700 fpm 215 m/min
Service ceiling: 6,900 ft 2,100 m

Range: 28 mi 45 km
Endurance: 25 min
Fuel capacity: 52 U.S. gal 196.5 l

Power plant(s): Two Hiller 8RJ2B ramjets rated at 45 equivalent hp (40 lb static thrust at 550 rotor RPM)

Role/configuration: Very light two-seat helicopter for tip-propulsion concept evaluation

Model 12-C/Army H-23C 1955

Length: 27 ft 10 in 8.47 m
Width (fuselage): 5 ft 0 in 1.52 m
Height: 9 ft 10 in 2.98 m
Rotor diameter: 35 ft 0 in 10.67 m

Empty weight: 1,643 lb 745 kg
Gross weight: 2,500 lb 1,135 kg

Top speed: 84 mph 134 km/h
Cruise speed: 76 mph 122 km/h
Initial rate of climb: 770 fpm 235 m/min
Service ceiling: 10,000 ft 3,080 m

Range: 138 mi 222 km
Fuel capacity:* 28 U.S. gal 106 l

Power plant(s): Franklin 6V4-200-C33
  six-cylinder horizontally opposed
  piston engine rated at 200 hp

Role/configuration: Three-seat
  light commercial/military helicopter

*Optional side-mounted auxiliary fuel tank
provides an additional 18 U.S. gallons (64
liters) of fuel

YROE-1 Rotorcycle 1957

Length: 12 ft 6 in 3.81 m
Width: 8 ft 4 in 2.54 m
Height: 6 ft 11 in 2.10 m
Rotor diameter: 18 ft 6 in 5.63 m

Empty weight: 300 lb 136 kg
Gross weight: 556 lb 252 kg

Top speed: 70 mph 113 km/h
Cruise speed: 52 mph 84 km/h
Initial rate of climb: 1,160 fpm 355 m/min
Service ceiling: 13,200 ft 4.025 m

Range: 166 mph 267 km
Endurance: 40 min
Fuel capacity: 2.7 U.S. gal 10.2 l

Power plant(s): Nelson H-63 four-cylinder
  two-cycle horizontally opposed air-cooled
  engine rated at 45 hp

Role/configuration: Foldable pilot-rescue,
  observation, and "small unit tactical mission" vehicle developed for Marine Corps

Model 12D/Army H-23D 1957

Length: 27 ft 0 in 8.23 m
Width (fuselage): 5 ft 0 in 1.52 m
Height: 10 ft 1 in 3.07 m
Rotor diameter: 35 ft 0 in 10.67 m
Empty weight (12D): 1,723 lb 780 kg
(H-23D): 1,787 lb 810 kg
Gross weight: 2,600 lb 1,179 kg

Top speed: 94 mph 151 km/h
Cruise speed: 83 mph 134 km/h
Initial rate of climb: 1,000 fpm 305 m/min
Service ceiling: 13,000 ft 3,962 m

Range: 274 mi 441 km
Fuel capacity:* 48 U.S. gal 181 l

Power plant(s): Lycoming VO-435-23A six-
cylinder horizontally opposed piston engine
rated at 250 hp

Role/configuration: Three-seat light commer-
cial/military helicopter; heated litter carriers
for H-23D air ambulance

*Optional side-mounted auxiliary fuel tank
provides additional 18 U.S. gallons (64 liters)
of fuel

Hiller 12E/H-23G 1959/1961

Length: 28 ft 6 in 8.69 m
Width: 7 ft 6 in 2.29 m
Height: 10 ft 2 in 3.11 m
Rotor diameter: 35 ft 5 in 10.79 m

Empty weight: 1,700 lb 772 kg
Gross weight: 2,750 lb 1,247 kg

Top speed: 96 mph 154 km/h
Cruise speed: 90 mph 145 km/h
Initial rate of climb: 1,500 fpm 458 m/min
Service ceiling: 15,000 ft 4,575 m

Range: 225 mi 360 km
Fuel capacity: 48 U.S. gal 181 l

Power plant(s): Lycoming VO-540-BIA six-
cylinder horizontally opposed air-cooled
piston engine rated at 310 hp

Role/configuration: High-utility light com-
mercial/military helicopter capable of
transporting 1,000-lb underslung load;
longest-produced and finest piston helicopter ever built

X-18 1959

Length: 63 ft 0 in   19.21 m
Wing span: 48 ft 0 in   14.64 m
Wing area: 528 sq ft   49.05 sq m
Height: 24 ft 7 in   7.50 m

Empty weight: 33,000 lb   14,982 kg
Gross weight: 27,052 lb   12,268 kg

Top speed (limited): 250 mph   400 km/h
Absolute ceiling: 35,300 ft   10,760 m

Range: 224 mi   360 km

Power plant(s): Two Allison YT40-A-14
    turboprop engines rated at 5,850 shp each;
    Westinghouse J34-WE-36 turbojet, rated at
    3,400 lb static thrust, for pitch control

Role/configuration: Two-seat transport-size
    tilt-wing VTOL research plane

Fairchild Hiller FH-1100/Army OH-5A
1963

Length: 29 ft 11½ in   9.13 m
Width (fuselage): 4 ft 4 in   1.32 m
Height: 9 ft 2 in   2.79 m
Rotor diameter: 35 ft 5 in   10.80 m

Empty weight: 1,396 lb   633 kg
Gross weight (normal): 2,750 lb   1,247 kg
(overload): 3,000 lb   1,360 kg

Top speed: 127 mph   204 km/h
Cruise speed: 122 mph   196 km/h
Initial rate of climb: 1,830 fpm   560 m/min
Service ceiling: 14,200 ft   4,325 m

Range: 348 mi   560 km

Endurance: 4.5 hr
Fuel capacity: 70 U.S. gal   265 l

Power plant(s): Allison 250-C18 turboshaft
    engine rated at 270 shp (317 shp takeoff)

Role/configuration: First-generation five-seat
    military light observation helicopter/civil
    executive helicopter

XC-142A 1964

Length: 58 ft 1 in 17.70 m
Wing span: 67 ft 6 in 20.57 m
Wing area: 534.4 sq ft 49.65 sq m
Height: 26 ft 1 in 7.96 m

Gross weight: 37,474 lb 16,995 kg
Max gross (VTOL): 41,400 lb 18,639 kg

Top speed: 430 mph @ 20,000 ft. 688 km/h
  @ 6,096 m
Initial rate of climb: 6,800 fpm 2,073 m/min
Service ceiling: 25,000 ft 7,620 m

Range: 450 mi 720 km
Fuel capacity: 1,400 U.S. gal 5,289 l

Power plant(s): Four General Electric T64-
  GE-1 turboprop engines rated at 2,805 shp
  each

Role/configuration: Small VTOL multiservice
  assault transport

Hiller L4 1965

Length: 29 ft 1 in 8.87 m
Width: 7 ft 6 in 2.29 m
Height: 9 ft 6 in 2.90 m
Rotor diameter: 35 ft 0 in 10.67 m

Empty weight: 1,960 lb 889 kg
Gross weight: 3,100 lb 1,406 kg

Top speed: 105 mph 169 km/h
Cruise speed: 89 mph 144 km/h
Initial rate of climb: 1,117 fpm 340 m/min
Service ceiling: 18,600 ft 5,670 m

Range: 260 mi 420 km
Endurance: 2.5 hr
Fuel capacity: 46 U.S. gal 174 l

Power plant(s): Lycoming TIVO-540-BIA
  turbocharged fuel-injected six-cylinder
  horizontally opposed air-cooled 340 hp
  piston engine derated to 310 hp

Role/configuration: High-utility four-seat
  commercial and executive helicopter
  incorporating L rotor and SAS developed
  for OH-5

*S*oldiers in a jeep communicate by radio with a litter-equipped H-23C during 1956 summer maneuvers at Ford Ord, California. Hiller Aircraft supplied the Army with more piston-powered light helicopters than did any other manufacturer.

An Army trooper on the ground watches a sharpshooter take aim high above the ground. The idea of "magic carpets" for crossing natural and man-made barriers— mine fields among the latter—appealed to the Army, which assumed sponsorship of Hiller ducted-fan development from the Navy in 1955.

Appendix B

Hiller Serial and Bureau Numbers[1]

U.S. ARMY:

Type	Serial No.	Quantity	Contract No.	Notes
YH-23A	50-1254	1	164	Stock UH-12 sold, fall 1949
H-23A	51-3969	1	177	
	51-3970/3976	7	183/189	
	51-3977/3982	6	199/204	
	51-3983/4018	36	205/240	
	51-15966/15967	2	112; 116	To USAF for evaluation
	51-15968/15969	2	124; 154	To USAF for evaluation
	51-15970	1	173	To USAF for evaluation
	51-16092/16141	50	246/295	
	Total	105		
H-23B	51-16142/16149	8	296/303	
	51-16150/16185	36	310/345	
	51-16186/16197	12	355/366	
	51-16198/16205	8	378/385	
	51-16206/16207	2	399/400	
	51-16208/16218	11	388/398	
	51-16219/16228	10	401/410	
	51-16229/16264	36	421/456	
	51-16265/16299	35	458/492	
	51-16300/16303	4	506/509	
	51-16304/16311	8	512/519	
	51-16312/16323	12	524/535	
	51-16324/16328	5	556/560	

1. Based on *U.S. Military Aircraft Designations and Serials* by John M. Andrade (Leicester, England: Midland County Publications, 1979), and other published serial listings.

Type	Serial No.	Quantity	Contract No.	Notes
H-23B	51-16329	1	562	
(cont.)	51-16330/16335	6	564/569	
	51-16336/16338	3	572/574	
	51-16339/16349	11	576/586	
	51-16350/16352	3	588/590	
	51-16353/16354	2	594/595	
	51-16355/16360	6	600/605	
	51-16361	1	608	
	51-16362/16364	3	610/612	
	51-16365/16381	17	615/631	
	51-16382/16404	23	633/655	
	51-16405/16406	2	657; 656	
	51-16407	1	658	
	51-16408/16413	6	661/666	
	51-16414	1	669	
	54-862/866	5	675/679	
	54-867/871	5	681/685	
	54-872/875	4	687/690	
	54-876/877	2	694; 693	
	54-878/880	3	695; 697	
	54-881	1	691	
	54-2915/2932	18	706/723	
	54-2933/2949	17	727/743	
	54-4009/4010	2	347; 415	Rebuilt for MDAP and Army
	54-4011/4012	2	416; 351	″ ″ ″ ″ ″
	54-4013/4014	2	352; 371	″ ″ ″ ″ ″
	54-4015/4016	2	346; 367	″ ″ ″ ″ ″
	54-4017/4018	2	354; 412	″ ″ ″ ″ ″
	54-4019/4020	2	413; 373	″ ″ ″ ″ ″
	54-4021/4022	2	374; 307	″ ″ ″ ″ ″
	54-4023/4024	2	418; 309	″ ″ ″ ″ ″
	54-4025/4026	2	308; 366	″ ″ ″ ″ ″
	54-4027/4028	2	349; 420	″ ″ ″ ″ ″
	54-4029/4030	2	305; 372	″ ″ ″ ″ ″
	54-4031/4032	2	414; 376	″ ″ ″ ″ ″
	54-4033/4034	2	350; 375	″ ″ ″ ″ ″
	Total	354		

Type	Serial No.	Quantity	Contract No.	Notes
H-23C	55-4060	1	749	
	55-4063/4066	4	753/756	
	55-4067/4070	4	758/761	
	55-4071/4075	5	763/767	
	55-4076/4080	5	771/775	
	55-4081/4085	5	779/783	
	55-4086/4092	7	787/793	
	55-4093/4100	8	796/803	
	55-4101/4108	8	805/812	
	55-4109/4116	8	814/821	
	55-4117/4124	8	823/830	
	55-4125/4131	7	832/838	
	56-2245/2250	6	841/846	
	56-2251/2256	6	850/855	
	56-2257/2262	6	859/864	
	56-2263/2268	6	868/873	
	56-2269/2274	6	877/882	
	56-2275/2280	6	886/891	
	56-2281/2286	6	895/900	
	56-2287/2316	30	904/933	
	56-4020/4021	2	893/894	To Spanish Air Force as Z.6-1/2
	57-6521	1	937	To Netherlands Air Force as O-36
	Total	145		
H-23D	55/4061/4062	2	750/751	
	57-2982/2985	4	938/941	
	57-2986/2996	11	943/953	
	57-2997/3050	54	955/1008	
	57-3051	1	1012	
	57-3052/3053	2	1010/1011	
	57-3054/3055	2	1014; 1013	
	57-3056/3057	2	1015; 1017	
	57-3058/3059	2	1016; 1018	
	57-3060/3061	2	1020; 1009	
	57-3062/3065	4	1021/1024	
	57-3066	1	1019	
	57-3067/3076	10	1025/1034	
	57-3077	1	1046	
	58-5398/5505	108	1047/1154	

Type	Serial No.	Quantity	Contract No.	Notes
H-23D	59-2675/2786	112	1155/1266	
(cont.)	61-3085/3114	30	1271/1300	
	Total	348		
H-23F	59-2787/2790	4	2125/2128	
	61-3218/3222	5	2167/2171	
	61-3223/3225	3	2230/2232	
	61-3226/3229	4	2242/2245	
	61-3230/3233	4	2249/2252	
	61-3234	1	2256	
	62-12507/12509	3	2283/2285	
	62-12510	1	2293	
	62-12511/12512	2	2307/2308	
	64-14850/14851	2	2297/2298	
	65-13069	1	2372	
	66-8039	1	2373	
	67-14867/14868	2		
	Total	33		
H-23G	61-3088/3217	130	1274/1403	
	62-3756/3831	76	1404/1479	
	63-9222/9371	150		
	[63-9524/9675]	[152]		Order canceled
	63-12765/12901	137	1480/1616	
	64-15108/15317	210	1617/1826	
	66-13106/13195	90		
	Total	793		
YH-32	53-4663/4664	2		Redesigned Hiller HJ-1 Hornet
	55-4963/4974	12		
VZ-1E	56-6944/6945	2		Hiller Flying Platforms
OH-5A	62-4206/4210	5		Hiller FH-1100 LOH prototypes (originally HO-5A)

U.S. AIR FORCE:

Type	Serial No.	Quantity	Contract No.	Notes
H-23A	51-15966/15967	2	112; 116	From Army for evaluation
	51-15968/15969	2	124; 154	From Army for evaluation
	51-15970	1	173	From Army for evaluation
	Total	5		
X-18	57-3078	1		Tilt-wing VTOL research plant

U.S. NAVY:

Type	Bureau No.	Quantity	Contract No.	Notes
HTE-1	125532	1	163	Evaluated at NAS Patuxent River
	128637/128640	4	179/182	Sold 12/15/50 through 9/28/51
	128641/128647	7	192/198	
	128648/128652	5	241/245	
	[129169/129184]	0		Preempted by Army wartime priority
	Total	17		
HTE-2	129757/129762	6	304/309	First HTE-2 sold 3/31/52
	129763/129771	9	346/354	
	129772/129781	10	367/376	
	129782/129791	10	411/420	
	134724/134743	20	534/553	MDAP to Royal Navy as HT. 1 (XB474/XB481, XB513/XB524) Last HTE-2 sold 5/1/53
HOE-1	138651/138653	3		Redesigned Hiller HJ-1 Hornet

TRI-SERVICE (ARMY-NAVY-USAF):

Type	Serial No.	Quantity	Notes
Vought-Hiller-Ryan XC-142A	62-5921/62-5925	5	Pre-production VTOL assault transports for evaluation

Appendix C

Museums Displaying Hiller Aircraft

Evergreen International Airlines Museum, McMinnville, Oregon
Two Hiller 12Es (one on extended loan to the Museum of Flight in Seattle, Washington)

Fleet Air Arm Museum, Yeovilton, England
Hiller HT. 1 (HTE-2)

Florence Air and Missile Museum, Florence, South Carolina
Hiller H-23C

45th Infantry Division Museum, Oklahoma City, Oklahoma
Hiller H-23

Fort Sill Museum, Fort Sill, Oklahoma
Hiller OH-23F Raven

Hiller Aircraft Museum, San Mateo County, California
UH-4 Commuter, UH-5B (NC-5 no. 3), J-10 (reproduction), 360, H-23A, H-23B, HTE-2, Hornet, HOE-1, YH-32 (prototype), YH-32 ULV (*Sally Rand*), Flying Platform 1, XROE-1, YROE-1, CAMEL (original company mock-up), OH-23F, L4, Ten99,

FH-1100, plus numerous original company models, power plants, and other small artifacts (as of this writing, this museum is closed awaiting preparation of a permanent home in San Mateo County, California)

International Helicopter Museum, Avon, England
Hiller 12-C (UH-12C)

Museum of Flight, Boeing Field, Seattle, Washington
Hiller 12E (on loan from Evergreen Museum), YH-32 Hornet

National Air and Space Museum, Smithsonian Institution, Washington, D.C.
Hiller XH-44, HOE-1 Hornet, Flying Platform 2, YROE-1 Rotorcycle (on loan to Naval Air Test and Evaluation Museum, NAS Patuxent River, Maryland)

Naval Air Test and Evaluation Museum, Patuxent River, Maryland
Hiller YROE-1 Rotorcycle (on loan from NASM/SI)

New England Air Museum,
Windsor Locks, Connecticut
Hiller OH-23G Raven

Oregon National Guard Military Museum
& Resource Center, Oregon
Hiller H-23

Pate Museum of Transportation,
Fort Worth, Texas
Two Hiller H-23Bs

Pima County Air Museum, Tucson, Arizona
Hiller 12-C (UH-12C)

Royal Netherlands Air Force Museum,
Soesterberg Air Force Base, Holland
Hiller H-23C

Royal Thai Air Force Museum,
Bangkok, Thailand
Hiller UH-12B (12-B)

Swiss Air Force Museum,
Dübendorf, Switzerland
Hiller UH-12B (12-B)

U.S. Army Aviation Museum,
Fort Rucker, Alabama
Hiller H-23A, H-23B, H-23C, H-23D,
OH-23F, OH-23G, two YH-32 Hornets;
Vought-Hiller-Ryan XC-142A

U.S. Army Transportation Museum,
Fort Eustis, Virginia
Hiller H-23B

[Note: This is a partial list as museum collections continue to grow. In particular, it is expected that many more Hiller H-23s will find their way into museums during the coming years.]

Notes

Introduction

1. Stanley Hiller, Jr., interview with author, 2–4 June 1988, transcript, p. 118.

Adventurous Beginnings

1. Interview with author, 2–4 June 1988, transcript, p. 7.
2. Ibid., p. 10.
3. Hal Risdon, "Hiller—Boy Aero Wizard," *Flying Aces*, March 1945, p. 33.

The Between Years

1. Today Page Mill Road is in the heart of Silicon Valley. In the field where the J-5 first flew stands the headquarters of the Hewlett-Packard Corporation.
2. Interview with author, 2–4 June 1988, transcript, p. 59.
3. Interview with author, 5 May 1990.
4. Ibid.
5. Cyclic control is achieved by changing the angle of individual rotor blades as they pass through the same area in their rotation above the helicopter. Pushing the control stick to the left, for example, locally increases blade pitch—hence produces greater aerodynamic lift—where needed to induce a roll to the left. The effect is similar to tilting the rotor above the helicopter, although with cyclic control the rotor's plane of rotation remains flat in relation to the helicopter.
6. Interestingly, Bell and Hiller both had stability-producing mechanisms in their helicopters, but Sikorsky did not. His unstable machines diverged slowly enough, however, for pilots to counter their inherent instability with corrective control inputs. The pilot work load of early Sikorsky helicopters was high, particularly during hover.
7. Scholer Bangs, "Hiller Copter Has Built-In Stability," *Aviation Week*, 15 December 1947, p. 25.
8. Ibid., p. 30.
9. Interview with author, 2–4 June 1988, transcript, p. 66.
10. William Flynn, "Helicopters Are Easy: Look Ma, I'm Hovering," *San Francisco Chronicle*, no date [1947].

Willow Road

1. Piasecki became Vertol Aircraft in 1956. Acquired by Boeing in 1960, it operated as the Seattle aerospace giant's Vertol Division until early 1988, when it was officially renamed Boeing Helicopters.
2. In fact, as observed by retired Bell vice-president Joseph Mashman, "The Hiller aircraft always outperformed us. We were always behind them." A noted helicopter authority, Mashman joined Bell in 1943 and has since logged over 16,000 hours of rotary-wing time in all makes and models of helicopters. Interview with author, 26 January 1990.
3. In 1951, Bell transferred its helicopter division to a new facility near Fort Worth, Texas. On 1 January 1957, this division became the Bell Helicopter Corporation, a wholly owned subsidiary of Bell Aircraft.
4. From a peak of $317 million in 1944, Bell Aircraft gross sales shrank to just $11 million in 1946.
5. *American Helicopter* 12, no. 10, September 1948, p. 25.

6. *Bell Aircraft News* 1, no. 1, 6–8 June 1952, p. 2.

7. Companies introducing new technologies and pioneering new markets often fail, whereas others following them succeed. Exhausted by the high cost of creating an awareness of and demand for a new product, the pioneer finds itself unable to compete in price with newly arrived competitors not burdened with comparable market-development costs.

8. Subcommittee for Special Investigations, House Committee on Armed Services, *Review of Army Procurement of Light Observation Helicopters*, 90th Cong., 1st sess., testimony of William D. Rollnick, 5 May 1967, p. 522.

9. C. Langhorne Washburn, "The First Nine Years," *American Helicopter*, January 1949, p. 11.

10. Interview with author, 10 February 1989.

11. Ibid.

12. Three HO3S-1s (Sikorsky R-5s) of the Navy's pioneering helicopter unit VX-3 arrived in San Diego, California, on 19 February 1948 ten days after leaving their base at Lakehurst, New Jersey. This 41-flight-hour, 2,600-mile journey was the first official transcontinental helicopter flight, but it actually followed a similar trip made some weeks earlier by a Navy captain, C. C. Marcy, commander of VX-3. This undocumented flight—made without fanfare as he blazed the trail to be followed—was in all probability the first helicopter crossing of the United States.

13. Interview with author, 4 June 1988, transcript, p. 121.

14. Stanley Hiller, telephone interview with author, 7 June 1990.

15. "Helicopter Unable to Help Injured Lad," no source [3 August 1949]; reproduced by United Helicopters in promotional compilation of rescue clippings.

16. Jay Demming, "Hallinans Knew He Was Safe with Me," *San Francisco Chronicle*, 5 August 1949, p. 3.

17. "Helicopter Rescues Hurt Hallinan Boy!" *San Francisco Examiner*, 4 August 1949, p. 1.

18. "'Copter Rescues Injured Boy," *San Francisco News*, 4 August 1949, p. 1.

19. *Hiller copter News* 2, no. 5, 15 May 1951, p. 3.

20. *HCN* 2, no. 3, 15 March 1951, p. 3.

21. Interview with author, p. 53.

22. Leo Bellieu to author, 20 May 1990.

23. Valérie André, *Madame le Général*, Paris: Librairie Académique Perrin, 1988, p. 138.

24. *HCN* 5, no. 3, September 1954, p. 3.

25. *BAN* (Texas Edition) 1, no. 4, 7 November 1952, p. 2.

26. Ibid., 1, no. 26, 11 September 1953, p. 1.

Tip-powered Helicopters

1. Interview with author, 5 May 1990.

2. The Aircraft Division of McCulloch Motors was formed in 1949 to market a small tandem-rotor helicopter to which the engine manufacturer had acquired rights. The McCulloch MC-4, as it was designated, was a revised version of the JOV-3, which was designed in 1947 by former Piasecki Helicopter employees.

3. *HCN* (Special Edition) 2, no. 2, 15 February 1951, p. 6.

4. John F. Straubel, "Sample Chapter Four," manuscript portion of proposed Hiller history, Hiller Museum archives, p. 31.

5. "Hiller Unveils New Jet Helicopter," Hiller Helicopters press release, 27 February 1951.

6. Elbert R. Sargent to author, 26 July 1989.

7. A 1951 Army order for a single-place helicopter capable of aerial delivery by parachute had already produced the pulse jet-powered American Helicopter XH-26, examples of which flew in 1952. Bearing a superficial resemblance to the Hiller Hornet, the XH-26—and other small tip-engine prototypes tested by American industry—failed to achieve service test production like the Hiller YH-32.

8. Straubel, p. 33.

9. Ibid., p. 43.

10. *Lockheed Horizons*, Lockheed Corporation, Burbank, California, 6th Edition, 1967, p. 66.

11. John B. Nichols, "The Application of Tip Turbojets to the Solution of Design and Operating Problems of Large Helicopters," reprinted from *Proceedings of the Sixteenth Annual National Forum*, Washington, D.C.: American Helicopter Society, May 1960, p. 11.

12. Straubel, p. 64.

13. Interview with author, 5 May 1990.

14. Ibid., p. 72.

The Mature Years

1. "The Navy Comes Up with a Real Flying Saucer," *Collier's*, 29 April 1955, p. 33.

2. Ibid., p. 30.

3. Ibid.

4. Interview with author, 2 June 1988, transcript, p. 26.

5. As witnessed by the Bell-Boeing V-22 Osprey, development of the tilt-rotor has in recent years been actively pursued. The tilt-wing, however, is again emerging at the time of this writing as the favored approach to high-performance, non-helicopter vertical flight.

6. Contemporary comment, George Bright to Stanley Hiller, Jr.

7. Jay Miller, *The X-Planes: X-1 to X-29*, Marine on St. Croix, Minnesota: Specialty Press, 1983, p. 126.

8. One had nevertheless recently been demonstrated. The Vertol VZ-2, a small turbine-powered research plane jointly sponsored by the Army and Navy, performed the world's first full conversion of a tilt-wing V/STOL aircraft in July 1958.

9. Named for its chairman, Dr. Court Perkins of Princeton University, this Department of Defense Ad Hoc V/STOL Committee surveyed past research and endeavored to chart a course for the development of operational V/STOL aircraft.

10. Interview with author, 4 June 1988, transcript, p. 129.

11. Ibid.

12. Sargent to author, 27 July 1989.

13. Promotional leaflet, "Marines' XROE-1 Rotorcycle," Hiller Helicopters, 2 pages [1957].

14. Other manufacturers were working on similar programs, but Hiller beat them to the punch. For example, rival Bell would announce a 1,200-hour dynamic system overhaul period for the Models 47G and G-2 helicopters in January 1958, an authorization extended in February 1960 to include its four-seat Model 47J Ranger.

15. Delford M. Smith to Robert Wagner, 1989.

16. Ibid.

17. Everett L. Barrick, telephone interview with author, 14 November 1989.

18. Smith to Wagner, 1989.

19. The seating configuration of the E4 in fact copied that of the Bell 47J, a 1956 all-metal executive version of the venerable Model 47.

20. G. F. Champlin, "Hiller Predicts Sales Increase," *American Helicopter*, April 1960, p. 6.

21. *Hiller Highlights* 2, no. 1, Spring 1960, p. 3.

22. Ibid.

23. Interview with author, 3 June 1988, transcript, p. 52.

24. "'High' Records Set Over Rockies," *Ag-Pilot International*, June 1983, p. 47.

25. "*Hiller Graphic: Vertical Flight News Pictorial*," Hiller Aircraft promotional pamphlet for Model Ten99 [1961], p. 2.

End of an Era

1. LOH Hearings, testimony of Stanley Hiller, Jr., 27 January 1967, p. 173.

2. Hiller to author, 20 May 1989.

3. More properly called the Senate Special Committee to Investigate the National Defense Program, this body—nicknamed the Truman Committee after its first chairman—came into being in 1941. Having sped America's wartime mobilization and saved billions of tax dollars, the Truman Committee was in decline when Senator Owen Brewster, its fourth and final chairman, took on Howard Hughes in 1947. The committee disbanded the following year.

4. The Hughes 269's rotor and dynamic components borrowed heavily from the small, experimental, tandem McCulloch MC-4 helicopter, to which Hughes had acquired the rights. It, in turn, was a revised version of the Helicopter Engineering and Research Corporation's JOV-3, a 1948 helicopter designed by former Piasecki engineer D. K. Jovanovich.

5. LOH Hearings, testimony of James A. Carmack, 5 May 1967, p. 483.

6. Report, technical evaluation of LOH proposals, U.S. Navy, as quoted by James B. Steele and Donald L. Barlett in *Empire: The Life, Legend, and Madness of Howard Hughes*, New York: W. W. Norton, 1979, p. 352.

7. LOH Hearings, testimony of Stanley Hiller, Jr., 27 January 1967, p. 173.

8. Ibid., testimony of Alfred B. Fitt, 25 January 1967, p. 8.

9. Ibid., testimony of Warren T. Rockwell, 27 January 1967, p. 167.

10. Ibid., testimony of General Herbert B. Powell, 24 May 1967, p. 561.

11. Ibid., testimony of Lieutenant Colonel Samuel R. Boyer, p. 557.

12. Ibid., p. 554.

13. Ibid., testimony of Donald Armstrong, p. 511.

14. Ibid., testimony of Rea E. Hopper, 23 February 1967, p. 320.

15. Ibid., testimony of William Rollnick, p. 515.

16. Ibid., statement of the Honorable Porter Hardy, Jr., p. 42.

17. Stanley Hiller, interview with author, 5 May 1990.

18. Ibid.

19. Rose Lesslie, interview with author, 6 February 1990.

Selected Bibliography

André, Valérie. *Ici, Ventilateur!* Paris: Calmann-Lévy, 1954.

———. *Madame le Général*. Paris: Librairie Académique Perrin, 1988.

Apostolo, Giorgio. *The Illustrated Encyclopedia of Helicopters*. New York: Bonanza, 1984.

Boulet, Jean. *History of the Helicopter: As Told by Its Pioneers 1907–1956*. Paris: Editions France-Empire, 1984.

Brie, R. A. C., com. *A History of British Rotorcraft, 1866–1965*. Yeovil, England: Westland Helicopters, 1968.

Brown, Eric M. *The Helicopter in Civil Operations*. New York: Van Nostrand Reinhold, 1981.

de la Cierva, Juan. "The Development of the Autogyro." *Journal of the Royal Aeronautical Society*, January 1926, pp. 8–29.

———. "The Autogyro." *Journal of the Royal Aeronautical Society*, November 1930, pp. 902–21.

———. "New Developments of the Autogyro." *Journal of the Royal Aeronautical Society*, December 1935, pp. 1125–43.

———. *Wings of Tomorrow: The Story of the Autogyro*. New York: Brewer, Warren and Putnam, 1931.

Dorland, Peter, and James Nanney. *Dust Off: Army Aeromedical Evacuation in Vietnam*. Washington, D.C.: U.S. Army Center of Military History, 1982.

Fay, John. *The Helicopter: History, Piloting & How It Flies*. New York: Hippocrene, 1987.

Gablehouse, Charles. *Helicopters and Autogyros: A Chronicle of Rotating-Wing Aircraft.*

Philadelphia and New York: J. B. Lippincott, 1967.

Gregory, H. Franklin. *Anything a Horse Can Do: The Story of the Helicopter*. Introduction by Igor Sikorsky. New York: Reynal & Hitchcock, 1944.

Gunston, Bill. *Helicopters of the World*. Combat Aircraft Library. New York: Crescent, 1983.

———. *An Illustrated Guide to Military Helicopters*. London: Salamander, 1981.

Harrison, P. G., et al. *Military Helicopters*. Battlefield Weapons System and Technology Series. London: Brassey's Defense, 1985.

Lambermont, Paul, with Anthony Price. *Helicopters and Autogyros of the World*. Foreword by Igor Sikorsky. London: Cassell & Company, 1958.

Lopez, Donald S., and Walter J. Boyne, eds. *Vertical Flight: The Age of the Helicopter*. Washington, D.C.: Smithsonian Institution Press, 1984.

McDonald, John J. *Flying the Helicopter*. Blue Ridge Summit, Pennsylvania: Tab Books, 1981.

Miller, Jay. *The X-Planes: X-1 to X-29*. Marine on St. Croix, Minnesota: Specialty Press, 1983.

Montross, Lynn. *Cavalry of the Sky: The Story of U.S. Marine Combat Helicopters*. New York: Harper and Brothers, 1954.

Morris, Charles Lester. *Pioneering the Helicopter*. Alexandria, Virginia: Helicopter Association International, 1985 (40th anniversary re-issue).

Munson, Kenneth. *Helicopters and Other*

Rotorcraft Since 1907. Rev. ed. London: Blandford Press, 1973.

Munson, Kenneth, and Alec Lumsden. *Combat Helicopters Since 1942*. New York: Blandford Press, 1986.

O'Leary, Michael, and John Guilmartin, Jr. *The Illustrated History of Helicopters in the Vietnam War*. The Illustrated History of the Vietnam War. Bearsville, New York: Rufus Publications, 1988.

The Piasecki Story of Vertical Lift, Pioneers in Progress for over Forty Years. Lakehurst, New Jersey: Piasecki Aircraft Corporation, 1967.

Pitcairn, Harold F. "The Autogyro: Its Characteristics and Accomplishments." *Annual Report of the Board of Regents of the Smithsonian Institution*, 1930.

Polmar, Norman, and Floyd D. Kennedy, Jr. *Military Helicopters of the World: Military Rotary-Wing Aircraft Since 1917*. Annapolis, Maryland: Naval Institute Press, 1981.

Prouty, Raymond W. *Practical Helicopter Aerodynamics*. Peoria, Illinois: PJS, 1982.

Rawlins, Eugene W., and William J. Sambito. *Marines and Helicopters*. Washington, D.C.: U.S. Marine Corps, 1976.

Riddle, Donald H. *The Truman Committee: A Study in Congressional Responsibility*. New Brunswick, New Jersey: Rutgers University Press, 1964.

Schafer, Joseph. *Basic Helicopter Maintenance*. Riverton, Wyoming: International Aviation, 1980.

Smith, Frank Kingston. *Legacy of Wings: The Story of Harold F. Pitcairn*. New York: Jason Aronson, 1985.

Steele, James B., and Donald L. Barlett. *Empire: The Life, Legend, and Madness of Howard Hughes*. New York: W. W. Norton, 1979.

Stein, Joe. *Lift*. Zig Zag, Oregon: Zig Zag Papers, 1985.

Taylor, John W. R. *Helicopters and VTOL Aircraft*. Garden City: Doubleday, 1968.

Taylor, Michael J. H. *Jane's Pocket Book, 20 Helicopters*. London: Macdonald and Jane's, 1978.

Taylor, Michael J. H., and John W. R. Taylor, *Helicopters of the World*. New York: Charles Scribner's Sons, 1978.

Thomas, Kas, and Jack Lambie. *The Complete Guide to Homebuilt Rotorcraft: The Essentials of Building and Flying Your Own Helicopter*. Blue Ridge Summit: Tab Books, 1982.

Tolson, John J. *Airmobility, 1961–1971*. Vietnam Studies. Washington, D.C.: U.S. Department of the Army, 1973.

Townson, George. *Autogyro: The Story of "the Windmill Plane."* Fallbrook, California: Aero Publishers, 1985.

Williams, Samuel C. *Report on the Helicopter*. New York: Brundage, Story, and Rose, 1955.

Wragg, David W. *Helicopters at War: A Pictorial History*. New York: St. Martin's Press, 1983.

Young, Arthur M. *The Bell Notes: A Journey from Metaphysics to Physics*. New York: Delacorte Press / Seymour Lawrence, 1979.

Index